"YOU'RE NOT STUCK—
YOU'VE BEEN POSITIONED."

Hea-
Avam to !

Endorsements

Whether speaking on radio or challenging audiences around the world, Gail has a unique ability to communicate a vision of hope regardless of life's circumstances. She inspires us to overcome challenges and realize our subsequent success can only happen through strategic choices and understanding of how to embrace our "position" in life. Her inspiring story and attitude of "do it!" will encourage you to maximize your impact from where you are...today!

>   Carl Anderson, EVP of Programming & News/Talk/
>   Sports Brand Management, iHeartMedia

Gail speaks in a way that makes you laugh and cry at the same time. She points out truth that hits home and brings you to an "aha moment" that changes everything.

>   Gayla Boyd, President, K & G Construction, Inc.

Wow! What a great way to achieve what most people chase their entire lives; purpose. Gail, through her own inspiring story, has shown us all how to convert our daily circumstances into difference-makers in the lives of others. How fulfilling is that?

>   Sam Caster, Founder, Manna Relief and EMSquared, a
>   social business.

I believe that Gail is "Positioned" to impact culture. She didn't allow herself to be "Stuck" in a perspective that limited her. *Stuck or Positioned: It's Your Choice* is about a mindset of pushing through limitations to accomplish the greatness within each of us. This book illuminates what can happen in your life if you have vision and determination to push through the obstacles that stand in your way.

>   Jay Hellwig, Vice President of Corporate Relations,
>   Generational Equity

Gail McWilliams has the gift of encouragement and motivation. She has overcome obstructions triumphantly and has embraced life in a way that makes everyone want to do the same. You will love this book and will fall in love with her. You will be forever changed for the better!

> Honorable Bob McEwen, Fmr US Member of
> Congress, Ohio

Gail's passion is undeniable and her vision clearer than 20/20. She will touch your heart and leave you knowing your journey has meaning and purpose.

> Pylar Pinkston, Financial Advisor, First Vice President-
> Investments, Wells Fargo Advisors

Gail is a woman with great vision, who has chosen a life of purpose that is not dictated by circumstance. This book (and her story) will encourage you to find your passion, pursue your purpose, and enlarge your vision for what is possible!

> Sarah Robbins, Speaker, Author, SarahRobbins.Com

This book is a tool for business leaders to reach beyond the status quo with a fresh perspective. Gail McWilliams reveals how setbacks can be strategies to reach your highest potential."

> Carrie Stumfall, Board of Directors, The Border Trade
> Alliance

Gail has a very unique style in sharing her vision and life experiences with others. Warm, witty, articulate best describes her presentations. I could sit and listen to her for hours on end and still yearn for more.

> Keith Thompson, President CEO, ABOX Packaging

Gail spoke to 200 of our executives, upper and mid-level managers. What an inspiration she is! She communicates in such an easy, open manner that you immediately feel connected to her in a personal way. She uses humorous examples of her daily life to challenge us to choose our attitude and take ownership of our destiny.

Marilyn G. Wood, CEO of Opis Senior Services Group

Gail McWilliams writes as she speaks – from her heart and from a wealth of life experiences that have produced measureless wisdom she takes great joy in sharing. No author I've read is more capable of encouraging others. *Stuck or Positioned: It's Your Choice* can have a major positive influence on you and your life choices."

Tom Ziglar, President and CEO, Ziglar, Inc

STUCK

OR

POSITIONED

IT'S YOUR CHOICE

GAIL McWILLIAMS

Stuck or Positioned
It's Your Choice

© 2015 Gail McWilliams

Written by Gail McWilliams
Cover Design by Bob Bubnis
Photography by Meshali Mitchell

Manufactured in the United States of America

Published by
Generations Global Press
www.GenerationsGlobal.com
"…beyond the horizon, around the globe,
and to generations yet to come."

For information, please contact
www.GailMcWilliams.com

ISBN: 978-0-9906707-4-2
LCCN: 2015945096

All scripture quotations, unless otherwise indicated, are taken
from the
New King James Version.®
© 1982 by Thomas Nelson, Inc.
Used by permission. All rights reserved.

TABLE OF CONTENTS

Acknowledgements

I may be the visionary, but others, whom I fondly refer to as my McTeam, are the ones who help me make it happen. Thank you sincerely to:

My faithful and diligent husband, Tony, who works around the clock to help me do what I do around the globe. Your constant support and first reviews, insights, and attention to details were priceless and essential, along with your help with late night rewrites and encouragement.

Linda McChesney Eisenmayer, whom I call my Content Developer. Your input is always insightful and colorful with suggestions and research that combine heart and facts. Also, a special thanks to Tom Eisenmayer for the knowledge and accuracy you lent to some stories in the book because of your career in aviation.

Bruce Barbour, for your expertise as my literary agent and dear friend. Your leadership and constant encouragement kept the project focused and a joy at every twist and turn of this journey. Your team's effort at Literary Management Group helped bring completion to the book, meeting every deadline on time as was promised.

My loyal assistants, Tonya Dagadu Asekhauno and Kimberly Morataya, who aided me with my every request for help, research, and anything I needed, as we crafted this new release.

My parents, Chet and Janet Moyers, who willingly and lovingly worked together to examine my manuscript, line by line. You are still amazing as a power team in your eighties.

Ryan Duckworth, for being my eyes and the Creative Director for the graphics and cover.

Lindey Duckworth, my personal shopper, stylist and director of my photo shoots.

A special thanks to all who graciously allowed me to use their story to help encourage others see life from a new perspective.

My amazing family who cheered me along the way and who remain at the heart of all I do.

Most important, the Author of my life, who has helped me see beyond the challenges and find the joy in the journey. Your abiding strength, wisdom, aid, and vision continue to cause me to live with purpose.

POSITIONED

"**C**ome on girls! You'll be late for school. Dad's in the car waiting on you!"

Our three young daughters brushed by me with quick hugs and last minute instructions. They shot out the door in a mad race to see who would get the prized front seat. Waving goodbye, I sighed knowing I had once again completed my morning obstacle course. Breakfast, rummaging through the unfolded laundry basket, collecting backpacks and homework, and sending the girls out with their dad were all-consuming. Calling out the open door I added, "Love you! Have a good day." I closed the door and leaned back against it. Now, I was finally able to release the tears I had fought to hold back since the early dawn.

That morning I woke up early with a sense of despair too deep for words and the dread of having to continue the nightmare my life had become. Though it was still early, I stood empty, with no reserve of strength to face the day. I walked slowly up the stairs to our bedroom. I locked the door behind me and collapsed on the floor with my face buried in the carpet, weeping from the very core of my being. A collision of emotions swarmed my thoughts. Disappointment, anger, frustration, pain, and grief swallowed my hope. Fear led the pack of devouring enemies that threatened my soul.

"God, how will I live from this point?" I cried aloud. I wept intensely for hours. I was stuck in a place I did not want.

My family was my entire life. A family that I thought I would never have, that doctors said was impossible. We had beaten the odds, and our prayers were answered, but it cost more than we ever imagined.

At first, my diminished eyesight seemed manageable because of the efforts of our close family who worked well together as a team. A combination of a childhood disease and changes in my body each time I was pregnant had done its damage through the years. The incremental loss of my sight was already our family's reality. However, that particular week—without warning—the blood vessels behind my eyes had hemorrhaged once again, threatening to rob me of what precious eyesight remained.

I could not be consoled in my dark prison of doubt and fatigue. How would I ever be the wife my husband needed? How would I ever be the mother my children needed? Blindness had no place on my life agenda. I felt trapped and forsaken. My questions had no answers, and my mind was weary from trying to make sense of it all. I did not even know *what* I believed any more. I lay there, unable to move, and sobbed.

After several hours, my tears stopped. There were no more. I stood up, physically exhausted and emotionally numb. Then a single line from a favorite psalm emerged. It was one I had tucked away in my heart years ago when my pathway started to dim. It quieted my soul. "Every tear I have ever cried You kept in Your bottle." I stood in silence when another thought surfaced. I whispered, "If blind for a season, then use it for good."

At that moment everything changed.

Nothing altered my eyesight, but my heart shifted. I believed in a God who could do the impossible. I hoped for a medical breakthrough. In spite of the tension between my hopes and the reality of where I was, I still had the freedom to not give up on any possibility. I found new courage. My quest now would be to find value in it all.

"But how would I manage?" I didn't know the answer, but a new resolve started to take form.

I wondered if I could use this new little light I had and direct it through an inner prism to reveal new perspectives and insights. Maybe I could see things I had previously overlooked. Maybe there were secrets to be had that even the sighted could not find. Maybe I would have the advantage to live life less distracted. At that moment I found the grace and courage necessary to step over an invisible threshold and accept the challenge to see more than is met by natural eyes. I determined I would take the time to see life differently.

With each step toward my newfound freedom, I was aware that I had been positioned—strategically positioned—to see beyond my own limitations and help the sighted see beyond theirs. In time people would remark, "You see better than I see!" What made the difference?

We live in a visual world where people can read all the signs, go where they want, and think they don't need anyone else. I realized I was positioned. People live life based only on what they see; I knew differently. Sadly, they often miss the big picture. I would be there to help guide them. I discovered a new source of joy because I once again knew my life had purpose. Real vision—which is not determined by mere eyesight—was birthed in my darkest hour.

Embarrassing situations taught me to laugh at myself and make them into life stories to share with audiences. My optimistic view of life translated into presentations and books to help others to see what I see. Teaching people how to run with confidence when they thought they were stuck with boredom and the mundane, was an added bonus to my life's work.

Even in moments of periodic sadness or times of tears, I was determined to find purpose and make the most of my circumstances. Though I was "stuck" with limited eyesight for a season, I adopted the vantage point of an eagle. The higher he soars the better he sees. My imagination grew and my drive increased when true vision was my goal, not just what I could see. My renewed outlook broadened my platform of influence far beyond my wildest dreams.

It is not uncommon to feel stuck in life. It happens to all of us. Each of us longs to hear words of encouragement in the midst of our lives. The truth is you are not stuck, but positioned for something greater than you imagined.

Stuck is not a place, it's an attitude. It's an environment where mental parasites breed hopelessness. This attitude deserves your disdain for the lie that it is. If you allow it to occupy space in your mind, it will fog your thinking and warp your perspective. As long as you *think* stuck you will *live* stuck. This debilitating attitude is not worthy of the life you are destined to live.

Elie Wiesel, Holocaust survivor and Nobel Peace Prize winner, made a statement to the world that resonates with me. His astonishing life story includes a horrendous ride in a packed cattle car as a fifteen-year-old to the infamous concentration camp in Auschwitz, Poland. He was a victim and eyewitness to multiple brutalities, senseless deaths, and inhumane conditions. With these and other atrocities in mind, including the loss of his father, mother, and younger sister he said, "Even in darkness it is possible to create light and encourage compassion. That it is possible to feel free inside a prison. That even in exile, friendship exists and can become an anchor. That one instant before dying, man is still immortal."

"Positioned" is an attitude acquired by a pro-active life, the key to each new day. This is a mindset where you are no longer a taker, but a giver; where your life has purpose and you radiate greatness. You are no longer a blip on the screen or just a part of the proverbial woodwork. You are strategically positioned to change the very atmosphere in which you find yourself.

I was stuck that day when I went into my bedroom to weep. When I made my exit hours later I was positioned. My circumstances had not changed, but my attitude had; and that changed my future.

Circumstantially, stuck and positioned are the same place. However, if you are stuck, there is no place to go. If you are positioned, the sky's the limit.

TRAFFIC

The Monday morning rush of traffic intensified as two major highways merged into one. Tony glanced at the clock on the dash to see if he could make it on time. Eighteen minutes were all he had left to make his important business appointment. Nearing downtown Dallas, anxiety mounted while traffic slowed to a crawl. Unexpected road closings, wrecks, and the express lane out of commission were no help. With irritation, my husband wondered why we had chosen to move our family to a small bedroom community outside the city limits. The morning traffic was always a mass of delayed people, with bumper-to-bumper exhaust filling the air, trapping fumes of anger in each vehicle.

Negotiating lanes to find a pocket to advance one more car length, Tony's vehicle halted near the downtown intersection of more super highways. Traffic helicopters hovered above, broadcasting warnings and updates of people going nowhere fast. Tony tried to find a way of escape, but there didn't seem to be any way out of this standstill. He was in the second lane of eight lanes of traffic—stuck.

One more glance at the dashboard clock confirmed his fear. He conceded. His first engagement to speak for the Ziglar Corporation was not going to happen on this Monday morning. Reluctantly, he made the dreaded call at 7:50 a.m. to report he wouldn't make the meeting scheduled to begin promptly in ten minutes.

"Hello. This is Tony McWilliams and I'm stuck downtown in traffic. I won't be able to speak to your staff this morning."

"Don't worry about the scheduled meeting," Mr. Ziglar's associate responded, "I'll cover for you today and reschedule you for another time." Relieved, but embarrassed and annoyed, Tony thanked him for his kindness and understanding.

Anything but comforted, Tony sat in unbelief at the needless hassle he had gone through, only to be stuck in Dallas traffic. Situated in the middle lane, he sat motionless between his home and the missed opportunity. Grateful he didn't face this stress every day, Tony wondered how anyone arrived anywhere on time.

Though cars started to move at a much-reduced speed, Tony was still pinned in his lane. The driver in front of him had slammed on her brakes and jumped out of her car into the oncoming traffic. Tony struggled to understand the horror evident on her face. He watched intently as the Hispanic woman opened the back door on the driver's side of her vehicle and pulled her little baby from the infant seat. Tony put his car in park and ran to help the desperate woman. In a sense of growing panic she looked first at her struggling baby and then to my husband. She spoke little English, and Tony knew no Spanish. The frantic mother searched in desperation between her native language and English to tell my husband what the problem was. Finally she blurted out two words he could understand—fever and seizure.

Tony quickly made his way back to his car in search of a quiet place to call 911. He looked for landmarks and surrounding businesses to help the emergency dispatcher pinpoint his location. He made the call and then ran back to the woman to assure her that help was on the way.

Without warning the woman suddenly placed the helpless baby into my husband's arms. Tony cried out to God for help. The paramedics were still nowhere in sight. He didn't know what to do. At that moment, while passersby looked on from their cars, a woman appeared and quickly told Tony how to hold a convulsing baby. While Tony assisted the infant, this medical professional attempted to calm the hysterical mother.

As the ambulance approached, vehicles pulled to either side and made a miraculous path for the emergency team to reach the scene. The baby was swiftly taken from my husband's arms and placed in the ambulance, where experienced paramedics moved with haste. Tony turned to find the mother. She was hurrying back to her car so she could follow the ambulance to the hospital. She stopped and looked at Tony with an expression of pure gratitude. Cars nearest the side of the road made way for the rescue team's speedy exit via the highway shoulder, and the ambulance sped off with the mother following close behind.

"What just happened?" he asked himself as he walked back to his car. He had completely forgotten his frustration with the traffic and his missed meeting. He called me to relay his story. Marveling, I said, "Tony, you weren't *stuck*, you were *positioned!*"

On my husband's calendar it read "corporate event." However, on a Divine schedule it read "rescue a life."

Every single part of your life has the potential to deliver valuable significance that could never happen without you.

Was Tony stuck that day or had he been positioned?

50-yard Line

remember well the first time I spoke in a football stadium. It was in Shreveport, Louisiana. As I was escorted to the 50-yard line to speak to the crowd in the stands, a thought came to me. I opened with my usual greeting in an attempt to connect with my audience. I know if I can win their hearts I will have their attention.

Within a few moments I highlighted my position on the field, "I find it interesting, and even profound, that where I stand today is where most people live—on the 50-yard line—standing between two goals, halted between two opinions. One goal represents a victory and the other a loss. There they stand afraid to move forward; fearing push-backs, remembering mistakes of yesterday, and paralyzed by indecision. They desperately wish someone else would come and play this game of life on their behalf. Overwhelmed, they are content to walk off the field and sit in the grandstands as a spectator." I asked my audience that day the same question I am about to ask you. "What would it take for you to get back on the field of life and play it with all your might?"

You have one life. You have this time in history. You are not an accident, no matter what the details of your story are. Embrace your position on the field of life. Advance forward.

Any parent with children in sports has surely laughed to watch young raw talent figure out the game they are playing. One young daughter made a sterling basketball goal—nothing but net—only to realize she had done so in the opponent's basketball hoop. Another little soccer player ran the entire field successfully and scored with precision. The crowd of parents laughed. She just scored the winning goal for the other team.

My son's little league highlights include this memorable play. He was caught in a squeeze between first and second base. He knew he must run like fire, so he ran off the base line hoping to find another way to second base. The cat and mouse game that ensued caused the parents in the stands to smile and laugh, as the opposing team went running after him all over the outfield. So much for the rules of the game.

However, when each little athlete realized their error in a blaze of embarrassment, they never made these same mistakes again. They actually *benefitted* from their early failures as their skills and athleticism grew by leaps and bounds.

Too many athletes hold something back from their game out of the fear of injury. This is unfortunate because the risk of injury is minimal when compared to the damage of forfeited dreams. In baseball, pinch-hitting is a strategy used by coaches, but no dedicated player wants to forfeit his chance to hit the ball. Winning athletes always prepare to give their best. Why should we settle for anything less in the game of life? Passivity is unacceptable. Make a difference. Join the team around you. Play with all your might to win. Have you wrongly assumed you simply won't make the cut? My plea to you is simple: Qualify yourself by working hard; be diligent to study what you need to know; seek out an inspiring coach; and reach for new goals.

I love hearing the life stories of successful people. Everyone experiences both victory and defeat in their lifetime. Michael Jordan did not make his high school basketball team his sophomore year because he was "too short and clumsy." Lucille Ball and Harrison Ford were told they would not make it as actors. Denzel Washington had divorced parents and was raised by his mother in Harlem. If he had not been sent to a preparatory school, he is certain he would not have survived his youth. The guys he hung out with at that time ended up with a combination of forty years in the penitentiary. At age thirty, Steve Jobs was fired from Apple, the company he founded, leaving him humiliated and depressed. He was hired back when Apple neared bankruptcy and Jobs then led them to new innovations. Henry Ford went broke five times. At age sixty-five, Colonel Sanders, the founder of KFC, had a small social security pension and a recipe for fried chicken he failed to sell 1,008 times.

These winners in the game of life didn't quit, and they were never stuck.

In the 2014 World Cup, the winning goal was delivered by a second-string player. Forward Miroslav Klose, the all-time top scorer in World Cup history, grew weary. The coach took him out of the game to rest while his substitute temporarily covered for him. His substitute, Mario Götze, received a pass from Andre Schürrle and volleyed the ball decisively with his left foot past an opposing player, arriving just inside the right post for a 1-0 victory in extra time. It was Germany's fourth championship.

Sometimes college football injuries leave teams decimated, but the best of teams learn to adapt to the changes created by injured players. Especially disconcerting is when a quarterback is taken out by injuries. The starting quarterback for Ohio State University injured his right shoulder in practice before the season began. The second string quarterback took his place, and there was talk that he could be in the running for the Heisman Trophy. Sadly, on the last regular season game he broke his ankle. The only games that remained were all playoff games. During the next three games under the leadership of a third string quarterback, Ohio State obtained victories over Wisconsin for the Big Ten Championship, over Alabama in the Sugar Bowl, and over the Oregon Ducks for the 2015 National Championship.

In the game of life there is no position you hold that is without value. We need you.

No one is stuck on the bench; that's merely a box seat giving you the best vantage point for improving your game. Pay attention. Apply what you learn there and your life will improve. You're in this game of life for the long haul, so enjoy it. Every step forward is a movement in the right direction. Aimless wandering won't do. Resolve to put an end to the futile cat and mouse chases of your past efforts, which only served to amuse your critics. Implement your strategy and advance intentionally.

In life, as in sports, the winners are not determined by the mere toss of a coin. Great achievements are realized incrementally over time, play by play, until victory is secured.

I was raised in St. Louis, and of course, I love the great athletes who have come from those teams. In particular, I am inspired by Kurt Warner's success story. Kurt would become a great football player, but he experienced disappointment along the way when others failed to see his full potential. Stories like his make sports fans wonder if winning is primarily about timing and the right team offer, or if it's about the character development of a man and his life message. Both proved to be true in the story of Kurt Warner.

After his college career, Warner went undrafted in the 1994 NFL Draft. Kurt's short career started with an invitation to a training camp with the Green Bay Packers, but during the preseason he was cut from the team. After Warner was released, the quarterback coach told Kurt he had enormous potential, but he was simply not ready for NFL quarterback status. His dream was to play on the NFL roster, but minimum wages and a new bride changed his short-term game plan. Kurt took a second job stocking shelves at a local grocery store. His lofty goals of touchdowns and football were suspended in order to provide for his household.

But his dreams never died. Kurt still hoped to get another tryout with an NFL team, but none were willing to give him a chance.

Warner turned to the Arena Football League (AFL) in 1995, and signed with the Iowa Barnstormers.

During the interim of life, family, and football, Kurt scored an eternal goal that changed everything. He accepted Jesus Christ as his Savior and has spoken openly of his faith from that time forward.

The experience he obtained in the Arena Football League was pivotal to his developing future. The game is different there. The field is smaller, the play is much faster, and quarterbacks must move, pass, and think more quickly. The experience stretched his already excellent abilities. In 1998, Warner was finally signed by an NFL franchise. He was sent to play on the Amsterdam Admirals in NFL Europe, where he led the league in touchdowns and passing yards.

Warner was eventually offered a contract as the third-string quarterback for the St. Louis Rams. The next year he was promoted to second-string. Warner finally became the starting quarterback when the first-string quarterback suffered an injury during the preseason. The head coach did not look for someone new; he announced that the whole organization would rally behind Kurt Warner.

Warner put together one of the top seasons by a quarterback in NFL history, throwing for 4,353 yards with forty-one touchdown passes and a completion rate of 65.1 percent. The Rams high-powered offense, run by offensive coordinator Mike Martz, was nicknamed "The Greatest Show on Turf," and registered the first in a string of three consecutive five hundred point seasons, an NFL record.

Sports Illustrated magazine featured Kurt on their October 18, 1999, cover with the caption "Who *Is* This Guy?" Kurt Warner was named the 1999 NFL Most Valuable Player at the season's end. He also led his team to the Super Bowl championship that year and was named the game's MVP.

From the wide-angle vantage point of the national football scene, it is clear to see the great success story in the unknown Warner who didn't make the cut, to eventually attaining MVP status. But when viewed through the telephoto lens of his personal character and diligent work ethic, he was already a champion with his family and community. Though Kurt Warner, the professional Super Bowl athlete, was inspirational on the field, he is even more so as Kurt Warner the man who kept his priorities straight.

Warner wasn't stuck; he was positioned with the privilege of everyday responsibilities that would launch him into future greatness. Warner simply trusted the process. He embraced the notion that he still had much to learn.

Are you willing to trust the process?

True greatness in ordinary, day-to-day life is separate from video highlights on the national scene. For most of us, our greatest accomplishments in life are rarely captured on video and re-played for all to watch. Our son, Connor, had just such an achievement during his senior year on the Prestonwood Varsity Soccer team. The team members were a close group of friends, and the comradery was awesome to watch, on and off the field. Our son was the goalkeeper. During one game the prevailing winds were a force that Connor believed could be leveraged to his team's advantage. The game was tied one to one. Earlier he told some teammates he planned to catch the wind just right and move the ball far down the field. "Get ready," he warned. Connor waited for just the right moment.

In the last half with the score tied, our son stepped up to the ball as he prepared to punt it down the field. Connor has an amazing ability to kick the ball a great distance, but the synergy of Connor's kick and the extra windy boost carried the ball much farther than normal. The opposing goalie ran too far forward because he hadn't figured the fierce wind into his calculations. The ball bounced once before sailing over the goalie's head and into the goal. Our team and fans went wild with joy. The other team was flabbergasted by this turn of events. Everyone saw it—except the referees. For some strange reason, they were faced in the opposite direction. Connor's goal never counted. No one could believe the injustice they had just witnessed.

Coach O'Neal, visibly irritated and determined, but in control, challenged the referees by telling them everyone saw Connor's goal except them. After the game, the opposing teammates congratulated Connor and confirmed they knew it was a legitimate goal and Connor's team should have won. The game ended in a tie.

Sports of any kind always include some forms of injustice. I have often quipped that possibly I should look into a second career and become a referee myself, since upset fans often think referees are blind. Inevitably, referees are not going to see everything on the field that fans see from the stands. The greater point is to move beyond the injustice and human error and not constantly review the replay in your own mind. Continue to improve your game of life and enjoy the satisfaction of a game well played and a life well lived, no matter who notices.

Play life to the maximum. Your game in life must be for more than mere men's applause. Those from whom you seek to get approval may seldom or never give it, but it does not mean your contribution is in vain. In the end, true accomplishments will not be so easily discounted. Use your current obscurity to your dream's advantage as you continue to master your game.

Game on. You're not stuck—you've been positioned.

HOPE

When I was a little girl I hated going to bed at night. My childhood era included record albums, black and white TV, and my parents who were like Ozzie and Harriet. Life was less complicated, with each day's routine like an episode of *Father Knows Best*, one of my favorite TV shows. Back then there were no cell phones, computers or advanced devices. Instead, imagination and harmless play satisfied. Everything seemed simpler then, but, of course, I was just a kid. I am sure my parents had more pressure than they felt they could manage at times. Not until I became a mother did I realize bedtime was a gift—for parents. After a bustling day, the sound of a quiet house is priceless.

If you are a night owl like I was, you learned to create ways to defy the clock. I was a secret agent of sorts and could quietly find my way around the house without the notice of my parents. I would sneak down the hallway and sit quietly on my pillow. By peeking my head around the corner of the closet door, I could just barely see the television set. However, a sneaky surprise always came from my dad who was just as sly as I was. He would move silently around the opposite end of the hallway to surprise me. When he crept up right behind me he would demand, "Get to bed, Gail!"

Our nightly routine became predictable, and my parents would inevitably win the tug of war, long after my set bedtime. Like bodyguards they escorted me to my bedroom. My stall tactics and negotiations were futile. They would place me in bed, turn out my light, and shut my door with a stern, "Now, go to sleep!"

But in the dark of night I would wait.

I had it timed to a science. Each night, when I thought my parents were long out of sight, the adventure would begin. I would spring up on my mattress and pretend it was my stage. I would use my hairbrush, flipped upside down in my hand, as my microphone. My fantasy adventure was to travel all around the world encouraging the troops with Bob Hope.

Bob Hope started entertaining our military troops in California in 1941. After that first United Service Organizations (USO) show he said, "It was love at first sight." The USO was one of several organizations mobilized to support the growing military as our nation entered World War II. Mr. Hope continued to do so throughout the war and beyond. During a fifty-year window he worked to boost the morale of soldiers in multiple wars, including the Gulf War while in his eighties.

Bob Hope mobilized the best of Hollywood to travel to military bases and outposts. Everywhere Hope went, the troops roared with laughter and applause. John Steinbeck, then a war correspondent in 1943, wrote of Bob Hope, "It is impossible to see how he can do so much, can cover so much ground, can work so hard, and can be so effective. He works month after month at a pace that would kill most people."

In addition to the shows, Bob Hope and his team visited the wounded soldiers in the hospitals. One famous comedienne was scolded when she became emotional at the sight of soldiers with missing limbs. Mr. Hope sternly reminded her they were not there to cry, but to make the moment light, giving these honored veterans hope of a better day.

Recently I watched some old video clips of his various shows. With artillery going off nearby, Hope put his quick wit to work saying, "General! Get them to quit this until the show is over." While watching, I marveled that I still sensed a kindred spirit as troops were given an encouraging word, a reason to laugh, and a season of refreshment, even when sounds of war loomed in the background.

People on *all* of life's battlefronts need encouragement. Some warriors wear business suits in CEO circles and strategize around boardroom tables. Others are educators, parents, public servants, or pastors. Though their battle strategies differ and their challenges vary, words of encouragement and inspiration infuse their lives. Parents are susceptible to unexpected battles on the home front where they may face a full time job at an office, and then another full time job caring for their families. They must face the stress and demands of both fronts. Teachers and professors continue to educate but are discouraged when they find a world majoring in the trivia of pop culture at the expense of character training and moral values. College students invest years studying for a degree only to face adulthood and working for decades to repay their student loans. And this assumes they can find work in their specific field of training. Leaders in politics, business, church, and social areas face a combative world that often results in weariness or apathy. Priorities and values get buried under an avalanche of busyness.

I still live the dream and I love what I do. I travel with hope, because hope always sees. It sees beyond all the battles, failures, and stresses of this life. Hope fuels the weary and empowers forward motion. It redefines circumstances and brings to the table a reason to keep reaching. It points you to more than you can merely see or imagine.

Hope renews strength and anticipates the dawn of a new day.

One of my favorite lines states, "If you are not living on the edge you are taking up too much room." I love the kind of leader who realizes that to not advance forward is to continually lose ground. Anyone can hang around like wallpaper, but leaders take calculated risks, initiate intentional action and make deliberate decisions.

Hope spurs action. Pioneer leaders of yesterday and the trailblazers of today know this is true. Visionaries all have one thing in common: they reach past their comfort zones to provide insightful leadership. Their visionary outlook is buoyed by the hope they know. *Hope* is the core of the courage that drives them on.

One spring, I was the closing keynote speaker at a conference in a large hotel near the Dallas-Fort Worth airport. I always finish by challenging the audience to face life's battles with renewed hope and vision. After I had finished, I walked back to my book table prepared to sign books. As I stood there waiting, my friend Eileen, a fellow speaker, approached me swiftly and said, "Come with me. I have some people I want you to talk to."

We walked briskly down the hotel corridor, and Eileen provided firm instructions. "Don't say a word until I tell you. I will speak first and then you."

Rapidly trying to keep pace with Eileen, I asked, "Who am I addressing?"

She said, "The hotel restaurant is filled with soldiers who are leaving tonight for Iraq."

"Do we have permission to talk to them?"

Turning on her heels she said, "Don't you get it? They may not come back!"

Slightly insulted, I replied, "Of course I get it! I just wondered if we had permission." As we neared the door of the restaurant I tried to come up with an explanation, should we be interrogated. I consoled myself that I would simply say I was visually impaired and I thought this was the conference. We moved to the center of the room as Eileen cleared her throat and said, "Excuse me. This is my friend Gail McWilliams. She has something to say to you."

I took a deep breath as I stood near a large table of soldiers eating their supper. It seemed I had no preparation for this new audience— or had I? Suddenly, I remembered the little girl standing on her bed with her hairbrush in hand, traveling around the globe with Bob Hope. I moved closer to the soldiers at the table, and others around the room looked on with curious attention. I placed my hand on the shoulder of the soldier nearest me. I then asked loud enough for the entire room to hear, "Hey Guys! Where are you headed?" Their chorus of response confirmed that they were, indeed, leaving for Iraq. The hotel was a private, comfortable place for them to hang out until their flight. The atmosphere was subdued. I stepped into the moment emboldened even more. I went on with my questions.

"What is your greatest challenge?"

Around the room came the same answer but packaged in different ways. All of them mentioned concerns about leaving home and separation from their families.

"I lost my eyesight having my children. I'm a soldier on the battlefield of another kind. I understand life costs something of great value." I could feel the stillness in the room as they were all focused on me. "Thank you for your willingness to deploy. Thank you for protecting us and our interests."

I told the soldiers about my childhood dream of traveling around the world with Bob Hope and encouraging troops. I said, "Guys, you're my first official troop. Come home soon." Then I asked if I could pray for them. As heads bowed, I simply said, "May the Lord bless you and keep you and make His face to shine upon you and be gracious to you. May He lift up His countenance upon you and give you peace." I went on, "God, protect them. Give them discernment and wisdom. May Your angels surround them and Your peace guide them as they go."

I knew I stood among heroes. I saluted to the room and said, "Gentlemen, from where I stand, I see generals all around the room. Come home safe."

Opportunities with all kinds of audiences have been afforded me before and since. But that day my childhood dream found its greatest fulfillment. I wasn't pretending anymore. I touched the lives of troops with an encouraging word.

The dream I had as a little girl provided the hope I needed in my young years to think something like that was even possible. The same is true for you. There is more possible in and through your life than you realize. Travel with hope. You're not stuck—you've been positioned.

FOG

A successful businessman drove down the highway one foggy Louisiana morning headed to his office on the opposite side of the Mississippi River. He had an appointment with a client, and he knew the commute would take too long if he restricted his travel to the highway. Instead, he planned to use the local ferry to cross the river. However, this particular morning the fog would frustrate his best efforts.

It was October 20, 1976. Bob continued to navigate the enshrouded, winding roads to the closest ferry crossing. As he pulled up to the gate in Reserve, Louisiana he realized he had just missed his ride. Impatient and angry, he decided to race to the next closest ferry crossing in Destrehan with hopes of crossing the river there. Bob determined to travel as fast as he dared, though it was still before sunrise. The pre-dawn fog had been dense but was lifting. Nothing seemed very safe that dim morning.

Eighteen miles later Bob reached the ferry landing. He could see red taillights of cars entering the ferry. He sighed with relief, thinking he had made it just in time. Then, unexpectedly, the barricade arm lowered right in front of his car. The ferry was full, and he would have to wait for the next one. Cursing the odds, Bob was stuck on the levy. His business appointment would have to wait. Bob had literally missed the boat.

It wasn't much consolation to be first in line for the next ferry. He anxiously looked at his watch. Cars filed in behind him. Bob was now trapped with no options. The time dragged on beyond all reason with no sign of the ferry's return. He fumed as he scanned the fog looking for a sign of the approaching ferry, but he couldn't see anything.

The ferry he hoped to board, the *George Prince*, left around 6:00 a.m. and the sunrise began five minutes later. He saw cars behind him back out and peel away. It gave him room to make his exit, too. He sped off, muttering, "I have the worst luck of anyone."

Airline Highway was Bob's only option, and this proved a further frustration as traffic was heavy. Finally he found his way across the river and made it to his office, hopeful that he had not lost his client altogether. Bob reflected that on any other day the road would have been perfectly clear. "Why then did I have to be delayed today?" he wondered.

When he finally reached his office his secretary was shocked to see him. "What are you doing here?" she asked. "We thought you were dead. Didn't you hear what happened today?

"*What?!*" came his irritated answer as he brushed by her to his office.

She continued, "An oil tanker broadsided a ferry this morning, and most were killed. There were only a few survivors."

Bob's face drained of color as he replied, "I'm going to my office and do not want to be disturbed." Shaken, Bob sat there in silence. He pondered the near mishap of his own life. Immediately, a simple phrase went through his mind, "Pay attention to the odds."

The accident, according to investigators, was not attributed to foggy conditions, but rather to the foggy minds of ferry operators with elevated alcohol levels. Mixed with the darkness of the pre-dawn hour, the results were fatal.

In time, Bob made some drastic changes for the good. His attitudes adjusted due to a transformation of his heart. Strangely, that foggy October morning marked the beginning of Bob's seeing the purpose of his life more clearly.

Fog is more than a ground-based cloud that sometimes hampers our transportation; it can also explain a mindset. It is the state when things seem out of focus and your way clouded and unclear. The great news about fog is that it's never permanent. In time it lifts, but when it is present you must be careful and cautious. In a fog there is more around you than what you can see up close. Just because you cannot see well does not make your world smaller or undefined.

During our visit in Brandenburg, Kentucky, I was escorted to a small Methodist church to speak. Brandenburg is quaintly positioned on the shores of the Ohio River, and this particular church is historic. It was a place of refuge during the Civil War, as the members of this historic congregation greeted the wounded soldiers with open arms. It was the essence of what every house of faith should be in a community.

While traveling to the town for my morning engagement, I reached for my sunglasses and said, "Why is it so bright today?" I noticed we were not moving very fast but didn't know why. My daughter Holly was driving, and she looked at me and softly said, "Hey Mom! You may not need your shades today. We're surrounded by fog. I can barely see the road." Our outlooks were different that morning based on different perspectives. Hers was external; mine was internal. Adjusting my sunglasses, I announced, "Holly, every day's a sunny day to me!"

I marvel at the stories of experienced pilots safely navigating their aircraft through treacherous storms. Trusting the gauges on the instrument panel is critical for safe flying. A pilot who insists on flying his airplane only by his instincts is not just over-confident—he's dangerous. Licensed pilots require many hours of additional training to become instrument-certified flyers. Throughout this arduous process, certified flight instructors always accompany the rookie pilots. A pilot in training dons a "hood," which looks like a baseball cap with an extra-long bill and side blinders. Their first job is to learn to rely entirely on the readings of the plane's built-in instruments, ignoring their natural perceptions. In adverse weather conditions pilots can lose their bearings and feel flipped upside down. But seasoned flight crews never second-guess their aircraft's instrumentation.

Back in November of 1963, a little boy, barely three years old, touched the world's heart in a memorable way. It was then, that John-John Kennedy stood at attention and saluted the casket of his father, assassinated President John F. Kennedy. As an adult, John F. Kennedy, Jr. worked as a lawyer, as a journalist, and as a magazine publisher. He even tried a stint at acting before marrying Carolyn Bassett in 1996. Somewhere along the line, John became a pilot.

On July 16, 1999, John and Carolyn, along with her sister Lauren, were all killed in a single engine aircraft. John, an eager young pilot with three hundred hours of fair weather flying experience but lacking his instrument rating, piloted the small plane. Earlier, Kennedy turned down an offer from a flight instructor to accompany him on this flight. The trio took off from Essex County Airport in New Jersey in the Piper Saratoga, flying across a hazy ocean. John's intention was to navigate the moonless night sky by using the shore lights and other landmarks. Young John checked in with tower controllers at Martha's Vineyard, but just eight miles short of the airport, their plane dropped off the radar screen. Radar data, examined later, showed the plane plummeting from 2,200 feet to 1,100 feet in a span of fourteen seconds, a rate far beyond the aircraft's parameters of safety.

Kennedy's plane was reported missing by friends and family members. Many civilians joined in the exhaustive rescue operation headed up by the U.S. Coast Guard, the U.S. Navy, and the U.S. Air Force. Five days later the mangled aircraft was discovered, and

26

Navy divers recovered their bodies. The National Transportation Safety Board concluded that the pilot's failure to maintain control of the airplane during a descent over water at night was most likely the result of spatial disorientation.

There's an old story told of two ships on a collision course. The captain of a battleship conducted routine maneuvers during unstable weather conditions. Concerned over the rapid deterioration of the weather, the crew on the bridge of the ship spotted an additional danger.

"Captain! We are faced with a great light coming towards us."

The captain stayed on the bridge to keep an eye on the developing weather. Now, aware of this unwelcome discovery, the captain asked, "Is it stationary or moving?" The crewmember confirmed it was stationary, which meant the battleship was on a collision course with the other sea vessel. Immediately, the captain ordered his signalman to message the ship, "We are on a collision course. I advise you to change course twenty degrees east."

The response came back, "*You* change course twenty degrees west."

Agitated with that response, the captain ordered the signalman to articulate another message, "I am a *captain*; you change course twenty degrees east."

Back came a rather defiant response, "I am a second class seaman, but you had still better change course twenty degrees west."

The indignant captain was furious! He shouted to the signalman to send back one final message, "I am a *battleship*. Change course twenty degrees east immediately!

Back came the pivotal command, "Change course twenty degrees west! *I* am a *lighthouse*."

Lighthouses are one of my favorite landmarks. Under the lighthouse keeper's skillful direction, their lights are beacons of hope in stormy conditions. They identify obstacles and direct ships to the desired course. Lighthouses are stationary for a reason. They are permanent fixtures anchored to the bedrock near the most challenging coastlines of the world. Yet, their charming simplicity hints of obsolescence and can cause seamen to take them for granted. Casual observers may believe them to be insignificant and old fashioned, but experienced sailors know their true worth.

Lighthouses are not available during the long haul of a transoceanic passage. They are only found near the end of one's journey, close to shore, where all the dangerous rocks and reefs can cause a ship to run aground. We can learn from the placement of lighthouses. However, we must alert ourselves to the natural inclination to be over confident or careless as we near the harbor of our goal, and our dreams nearly in hand. Carefully stay the course in wisdom. Open yourself to the counsel and assistance of those who stand as lighthouses, and who can guide you through potential dangers.

Are you attempting to live life without restraint or without belief in absolutes? Do you pride yourself in being your own self-appointed captain, and no one can steer you differently? I want to emphasize that the position of "captain of your own soul" is limited and overrated. Wisdom, truth, and universal principles are guiding lights that shine on life's rocky seashore, helping us navigate the rugged twists and turns near the shoreline of our dreams.

No matter where you are in your journey, life requires course corrections. When a spacecraft is launched from its launch pad, a countless number of course corrections are made in flight before arriving at the destination. Neither the launch pad nor the intended destination is negotiable. However, many course adjustments can occur between the two. If an adjustment is not made within moments of the slightest deviation, the spacecraft will not only fail to arrive at its destination, it also will burn a great deal of fuel getting back on course. Worse yet, if not corrected at all, the spacecraft could miss its destination by thousands of miles.

Sometimes a small alteration, or course correction, in our path keeps us steered in the right direction. There is nothing to fear unless you are stubbornly unwilling to make the needed changes. You've already taken off to new heights. Focus on the goal, make needed adjustments; don't be distracted by the fog or the unfamiliar. Navigate the unknown by depending on the instrument panel of higher wisdom and unchanging principles.

I once spoke at a gathering in Steamboat Springs, Colorado. The audience had the joy of looking out a huge window behind the podium where I stood. The snowcapped mountains were framed in all their glory. All I could do was trust that the audience could enjoy this vista and listen to me at the same time. As I continued to speak, I envisioned skiers racing down the mountain behind me as the snow fell. I encouraged my audience to live with limitless vision. During my opening comments I put my hand on my hip and said impulsively, "You all are spoiled rotten. You get this beautiful view and the grandeur of this incredible mountain."

Several spoke up from the audience and said, "But, the mountain is covered by clouds today."

Laughing, I continued with a bit of sarcasm, "You visual people are high maintenance. You *know* as well as I do there is still a mountain behind that cloud covering."

They laughed, seeing the vision I offered.

We often focus on the overcast moments of our lives—on this momentary covering—instead of what lies behind it. The mountain is symbolic of our deepest purpose defined by the Creator. It remains steadfast even when obscured by fog or socked in by extreme weather conditions. Our most common "cloud coverings" are past failures, persistent obstacles, and present challenges. Together they work to deter you from the climb to reach the top of your potential. But you must remember: it's just a cloud and ever so temporary. Why does it capture your attention so easily, more than the real goal? It is time to course correct. Refocus on your destiny.

Our second child was born four weeks prematurely, and spent the first ten days of her life in a neonatal unit. The medical staff feared a possible lung disease. I was still hospitalized, as well, recovering from her traumatic birth. The neonatal center was a one-hour drive from our home, but my husband drove back and forth to the hospital to visit us every day. One morning the fog was intense and visibility nearly nonexistent. As Tony inched along the super highway he wondered how he would make the trip safely. But he kept his family firmly positioned in his mind. Then, in a gentle way, he was comforted. A tender prompting resonated in his soul and said, "Move forward in the light you have."

The same is true of our lives. No one sees the full picture of an entire life. But, regardless of your circumstances, you must walk in the light you have now. Greater visibility will come in time. Confusion can cloud your way. Doubts are hazy spots, indeed. Disappointments threaten to obstruct the view. Life's conditions are ever changing and unpredictable.

Keep sight of your preferred destination and enjoy every inch of the way. If you must, course-correct. You're not stuck—you've been positioned.

GRATEFUL

The power of gratitude opens your eyes to see what you may have taken for granted or what you overlooked. It is also a vital key to not feeling stuck.

Dennis Prager is a syndicated talk show host who has dedicated most of his life to the study of happiness. He has given one radio show a week for the last several years to discussions on happiness, and he has written a book on it as well entitled, *Happiness is a Serious Problem*. He states, "Because gratitude is the key to happiness, anything that undermines gratitude must undermine happiness. And nothing undermines gratitude as much as expectations." In another passage he says, "The more we expect, the less happy we will be because the more we expect, the less grateful we are for what we receive. And ingratitude is the mother of unhappiness."

If only we had eyes to see the beauty of each season and trust the process in motion. What if our setbacks were viewed as inseparable parts of our expeditions to higher summits? What if valleys were treasured for the fertile soil from which the world is fed? What if obstacles are stepping-stones to creativity? What if losses are the eternal currency exchanged for new depths of understanding and empathy? What if awkward moments were a personal reality show to create memories extraordinaire? What if our conflicts were embraced for the incredible learning opportunities they contain? What if…?

There's a pattern here. Each situation and circumstance of your life is priceless and is a cause for gratitude because something is gleaned from each to make your life better. And yes, even happier. Mr. Prager believes happiness is a moral obligation. He points out that happiness is one of the core values of the Declaration of Independence. Our forefathers believed that there's everything right about life, liberty, and the pursuit of happiness. People who choose happiness contribute to the strength and health of a nation and its communities. Those who choose unhappiness create undesirable environments for themselves and others. Consider the effects of an unhappy parent on a child, or an unhappy child on parents, or an unhappy spouse on a marriage. Consider the effects of an unhappy coworker on the morale of a workplace.

What have you overlooked on your journey? Unhappiness puts you in agreement with stuck. Exchange your grumblings for gratitude.

One autumn morning we traveled by car to San Antonio, where I was scheduled to speak that evening alongside the Governor of the state. On the way there, my husband pointed out the corporate headquarters of Medtronics, a medical supply company. I am a grateful beneficiary of their research and innovations, as their team of scientists and engineers designed my pacemaker. I like to tell people, "This heart device has not only extended my life, it has also made me bionic!" I am grateful for every day it has added to my life—and am thankful to be on my second ten-year battery.

Just then, my grateful heart gave me an idea. I blurted out to my husband, "Pull in the parking lot!"

Tony said, "What about the Governor and your engagement tonight?"

I replied, "We have a little time to stop for a few moments." After all these decades of marriage, my husband is rarely surprised by my sudden impulses. After all, I just had one thing I wanted to do. The headquarters were brand new and quite large. We turned into the main parking lot and were met immediately by a security guard. He came to my window.

"Sir, my name is Gail McWilliams. I am in town to speak tonight with the Governor. I just stopped by to say thank you for all you do. Because of what you do, I get to do what I do—encourage people all around the world."

It was obvious I had caught him off-guard. He hesitated as he studied my face before saying, "You're welcome." Now, it was his turn to surprise me. With a smile on his face he asked, "Would you like to come in?"

Moments later we were escorted into the beautiful lobby. The guard took me to the receptionist's desk. I introduced myself once again and briefly mentioned the evening's engagement in San Antonio and why it was important for me to pay a visit. I then said, "Thank you for all you do. Because of what you do, I get to do what I do—all around the globe."

The young receptionist giggled, "You're welcome." She then quickly added, "Would you like to take a seat?" I sat down, eager to see what would happen next.

The security guard, my new friend, said, "I will be right back. I have someone I want you to meet." Suddenly, I loved this unconventional curve in my journey. My original intent was to practice an act of random thanksgiving, but gratitude was clearly taking on a life of its own. The guard soon returned with another gentleman he had brought out to meet us.

"Hello." He said. "I am the CEO of this division of the company." His name was Jeff, and he insisted I call him by his first name. I delivered my message of gratitude once more.

"Would you like to come to my office?" We spoke easily, as though we had merely arrived for a scheduled appointment on his calendar.

"Yes! I would love to talk more."

We took the elevator to the top floor and followed Jeff into his office where we had a lively conversation like old friends. I inquired about their company and employees and also asked about new medical research and new products. Jeff brightened as he spoke proudly of their accomplishments and the many who have been helped by their efforts. Once more I thanked him.

He asked about my life and my career and sat attentively while I openly shared my journey so far. Then, sensing the time passing too fast, I started to work toward my closing by simply stating, "Jeff. Anyone could have your job, but they don't. It's yours. And, if it's yours, then you must be the man for this hour. Seize it all." Then Jeff thanked me for my words of encouragement and the living proof I offered that their diligent efforts and products were changing the lives of people.

As I stood to move towards the office door, I turned to say, "Oh yes. There is one more thing." As he looked on with curiosity, I spoke a blessing over him, "May the Lord bless and keep you and make His face to shine upon you." He appeared moved and asked if he could give me a hug. Our interchange was priceless all because of a small gift of thanks for a job well done.

My prescheduled appointment that day was with the Governor, but my unexpected twist filled with gratitude was a bonus. Everyone who is attentive to the world around them will find similar opportunities to touch hearts and encourage others. I have never stopped by any other corporation since that day, in case you think I regularly stalk executives. That evening I simply followed my heart and found rich treasure in the experience. This is one of the secret ingredients for a life filled with anticipation, awe, and wonder.

Once I was challenged to make a list of all the people who helped me get to where I am today. The list was lengthy and filled with divine connections. Why don't you try it yourself? Think how long the list would be if you were to write down the names of all those who have trained you, connected with you, helped you, and were sincerely interested in you. Give thanks for them all. Thanksgiving is more than a holiday—it's a lifestyle.

One night our flight into Dallas was delayed past midnight. When we landed and deplaned, a groggy group of passengers moved quickly to claim their luggage before heading home to bed. To avoid the scurry, I stood off to the side. My husband grabbed our bags and suggested I wait for him while he went to get our car. In short order, the bustling airport abruptly hushed. I stood alone in the eerie silence. I felt vulnerable as I pondered what I would do if I needed help. I wasn't necessarily afraid but still considered what I would do as a blind woman when standing alone with no escape or help. Just then, I heard the heavy footsteps of a man coming towards me. I decided to look like I was on the phone and looked out the large windows. Truthfully, I really did not know if I was actually near a window. It could have been a wall for all I knew. Still, I felt good about my stunning performance. I could hear the man come closer, and then he stopped a few feet away. I listened to see what he might be doing in such close proximity to me.

It did not take long to vividly see the man's agenda. I heard him lift a hinged top as he pulled out a liner from a garbage can. I had no idea where I stood until then. He grunted as he lifted the bag and then twisted the top and tied a knot. Sighing, he dropped the bag on the floor. Next, he shook out a new liner and placed it in the receptacle. Then he closed the lid to complete his task. As he was finishing the job I decided exactly what I would do.

Turning toward the man, I said, "Excuse me, sir." He did not respond. When you cannot see, quiet people drive you nuts. I repeated my line louder. "Excuse me, sir."

Finally, he answered roughly, "Yes?"

"Thank you for what you do. It makes a big difference."

He laughed and said, "Lady. I'm just doing my job."

"Yes and it makes a big difference. Thank you."

On Veteran's Day I love to call my dad and others who have served in the military to thank them for serving our country. At Christmas I thank people for the gift they are to me. On the birthdays of those I cherish, I celebrate their life and thank them for the asset they are to this world. I have even told people to pass on my personal thanks to their parent for giving birth to such a great person.

I love to thank people in the service industry, wherever I find them. I tell them they are a huge asset to their employer. Sometimes I have even called for the manager to thank them for hiring such a great addition to their business. I smile as I sometimes suggest they get a raise. My goal is to express gratitude to whomever I can. In times of gratitude you will not feel stuck, but joyful. Gratitude combats self-centered living. I thank my parents often for giving me life because life is a gift.

I was coaching a disgruntled wife about her twenty-year marriage that had grown cold. I suggested she begin thanking her husband on a daily basis for the hard work he did. At first she thought it would be insincere until she realized how ungrateful she had been throughout their marriage. She saw only her needs and overlooked his desires. Within a few short weeks, their marriage took a turn for the best. The couple started showing interest in each other again and re-engaged in the lost art of conversation. He had a new reason to come home every night and she anticipated his homecoming. Soon, expressing her gratitude for the simplest things became an ingrained habit. And once her marriage was restored, she expanded her attitude of gratitude to others in her life that she had taken for granted.

When our children were younger they used to travel with us and sing in concert with one another. On one occasion, we had just returned home after a road tour and decided to treat ourselves to a buffet at one of our favorite restaurants. Every bite was great and satisfying. Afterwards, a bus boy came by to clear our table. That's when I asked for the manager.

The boy looked wary, like he might be in trouble. When the manager approached us, he was a bit defensive and walled off. I am sure he expected a complaint or demand. I said, "Mr. Manager, we have something to say to you." I glanced at our children with a look they knew well. We broke out in four-part harmony with a song of thanks for a great meal. The manager stood looking at us with tears flowing down his cheeks. He said, "This is the first time I have ever been thanked for a meal."

Another time, the children were with me at my doctor's appointment. Dr. Soler is a renowned endocrinologist. He aided us in maintaining our high-risk pregnancies and I will always be grateful for his care. Doctors do not usually linger long in the examination room, so I talked fast. "Dr. Soler, my children need to talk to you this afternoon. Can you wait one minute?" He agreed, and the nurse called in the children.

"We all have something to say to you."

The children joined me in melodious harmony, singing a song of thanks. Tears welled in his eyes as he listened to our miracle family thank him for a job well done. I will always love that man with all my heart.

My niece, Megan, once wrote the ultimate thank you note while she was a medical student at the University of Washington. At the end of the first year, the students have a memorial ceremony for the cadaver that had been assigned to them. The family of the cadaver is invited to attend the ceremony. Megan was selected to give the tribute. She read the following letter she had written:

Dear Ms. X,

I will admit that when we first met, I tried to pretend you weren't real. I tried to imagine you were simply a model. Perhaps colder, wetter, more squishy than the average plastic model, but a model nonetheless. You were only a "cadaver," only a "body"—a word I clung to for its distance, its objectivity.

But you have made it impossible to keep my distance. We have spent countless hours together, harried class sessions, and lonely Saturday nights under the unforgiving fluorescent lights. I have bent low over your stillness, searching for mysterious structures, while my heart beats inches from your quiet one. And over the last few weeks I have gradually felt my detachment give way under the weight of my wonder and the connection I feel toward you.

I have come to notice the freckles under my scalpel. I like to imagine you got them sunbathing in Bermuda or from years of horseback riding under the fierce Montana sun. I think that your ribcage is not merely a collection of intercostal muscles, membranes, and pleura; it was what heaved and panted when you ran, it was squeezed in hugs from your grandchildren and garbed in your Sunday best. When I removed your left breast, I felt a deep female pang within my own body. This structure, lactiferous glands and fat globules, brought you pleasure in your life; it breastfed your children and filled out the neckline of a long-ago prom dress. When I traced your brachial artery down your cold arm, I wondered who the last person was to hold your hand. I have held your lungs. We will never have a conversation, but I have touched the tissues with which you took your first breath…and your last.

Yes, you are a body. But there is nothing "only" about it.

Perhaps there are those who would say a doctor (and a first year medical student) should hold on to her detachment. I disagree. You have given me yourself, the body in which you lived for 76 years. You have allowed me to probe and poke and slice the very things that made you, you. What your body has taught me will form the basis of every medical decision I make as a doctor. When I palpate the abdomens of my future patients, it is your organs I will picture. When I press my stethoscope to warm chests, I will remember holding your small heart in my turquoise gloved hands.

So, you deserve more than my objectivity. I owe you more than detachment. As I continue to learn from your body, I promise to hold onto my sense of wonder and my empathy. I will never look at you as simply a collection of tissues and systems, just as I could never consider my patients to be compilations of lab tests and symptoms. You were a person. My patients are people. And it is both impossible and undesirable to divorce anatomy from humanity.

For this lesson—and for countless others—I will thank you for the rest of my life.

Megan

Look at all the people around you and how much they enhance your life. Thank them for all they do; it makes a big difference. You're not stuck—you've been positioned.

SEEDS

One of the best ways to get over feeling stuck is to give something away. There's nothing like getting involved in the business of blessing others to give your life a renewed sense of purpose. Giving is addictive, and life is good when you also consider others. Have you ever heard someone say, "When I get my first million, then I will give to other causes?" Yet, the personal satisfaction you hope to reap later in life can start today, even if times are lean. Your life is like a big bag of seeds waiting to be planted, watered and cultivated.

Everyone should have a friend who is a farmer. Mine is Gary from Minnesota where he farms over 3,000 acres. Often I talk with Gary about my favorite concept, seedtime and harvest. It is fascinating to me that the life of a seed is perpetual. Nowhere else in nature has so much potential been packed into such a small vessel. Consequently, the bountiful harvest that comes from seeds is beyond our calculation and imagination. A seed continues to give as long as it is planted. The greatest potential of growth comes from planting the right seed in good soil.

One spring, Tony and I were making plans to travel to Spain where I had been invited to speak fifteen times in eighteen days. We organized a team of six to travel with us. Our ambitious itinerary included traveling two thousand miles through the countryside with diverse meetings in various regions. My interpreter was a young woman by the name of Raquel, a Spanish native, perfectly equipped to help me articulate my message of hope, life, and vision.

Shortly after I accepted the invitation to tour Spain, Raquel presented us with a visionary challenge—to have two of my books translated into Spanish. Though this was a costly idea, it would be doable if we all worked hard and fast. Our learning curve was unusually steep because this was our first international publication. We had to secure a printer, negotiate prices through a translator, work out the timeline, and find a meeting point once we arrived in Spain where we could pick up five hundred copies of each of my two books. The really hard part was that we were still trying to figure out how we could raise the money to print the books and cover all of our expenses for the trip. At times I felt overwhelmed and wondered if we could complete all the tasks at hand.

Nothing surprised me more than the day I received a letter in the mail from a grain company in West Central, Minnesota. It contained a check for the exact amount needed to fully fund the printing expenses. I wondered if it was connected to my farmer friend when I read the name of the grain elevator on the return address. Tucked in the envelope was a short handwritten note that told the beginning of the story:

"Dear Tony and Gail, Congratulations! You've just made your first corn sale. You sold 1,600 bushels of #2 yellow field corn at a price of $3.30 per bushel. Less the discounts, this netted $5,047.20."

Gary explained the behind-the-scenes details of this agricultural venture. They planted three-and-a-half fifty-pound bags of seed corn, containing 80,000 kernels per bag in eight acres of land, and that seed produced 1,600 bushels of marketable field corn. Later, I learned that with the use of his satellite-guided tractor, it took only twenty minutes to plant these seeds in those eight acres of fertile soil. The profit was the *exact* amount we needed to impact the nation of Spain.

When our team arrived in Spain, we eagerly met the printer and collected our supply of books. During the next eighteen days, we distributed one thousand copies throughout that nation through sales and as gifts. Those profits subsidized our immediate expenses abroad. In addition, we were enabled to generously sow the seeds of hope and encouragement. The Minnesota seeds took on a new international form and continued to produce through our Spanish friends who now had something tangible to share with others. I am delighted to report some books were taken from Spain to other nations.

Later, when I asked my friend about the day he was planting seed, I inquired why he designated those eight acres for us. Beyond his generous nature, he felt compelled to give a portion of his seeds to someone who could do more with them than he could. I imagine he had days when he felt stuck in the fields, doing the mundane work of planting, cultivating, and tending his crops. I asked if he had anticipated the harvest those seeds would produce, let alone the impact his efforts would have on strangers in a nation he had never visited. He answered that every farmer anticipates a harvest, but you never fully know if your calculations are right. You simply plant and hope.

Our lives are like seeds with a harvest beyond our comprehension. A seed of kindness is a gift to someone who is having a bad day. A smile is a seed to someone who has lost their joy. A hug is a seed to someone who has forgotten they are loved. Our money is a seed, especially when it's given to someone in need. The warning is not to consume our seeds fully but to reserve a portion to sow into the lives of others. The life of a seed is endless. I love what my husband says when he states, "You can count the seeds in a single watermelon, but you can't count the watermelons in a single seed." The only way the legacy of seeds is stopped is when we quit planting our seed altogether.

While writing this chapter I called Gary. He was out in his field. He and some hired hands were walking between the rows of soybeans with common garden hoes in their hands. This is called "walking beans" for short. It is a concerted, labor-intensive effort to uproot volunteer corn and innumerable varieties of weeds that threaten to rob the soil's life-giving nutrients. Each weed carries the potential of an unwanted invasion that could easily take over a field of precious crops. Row by row, with just a hoe in hand, my friend was battling his crop's prolific enemies.

Seeds of greed empower self-centeredness and opportunities are overlooked and aborted. No wonder a selfish person feels stuck. Their bag of seeds is self-consumed with no hope of a harvest. If negativity robs the necessary nutrients from people attempting to dream big, and if words of the destructive type undermine others and steal from the common good, then why not use words that scatter seeds of encouragement and inspiration instead? Consider the power of words and the kind of harvest that they will one day produce.

An ugly mood is an unwelcome weed, which threatens to uproot someone else's positive outlook. Critical words drain encouragement and enthusiasm from the lives of all those within earshot. A narrow view can obscure the view of visionaries in your midst. However, seeds of encouragement and inspiration spoken from a caring person can put them on a more successful path where nothing is out of reach. Life and death really *are* in the power of the tongue.

It is vital to find a way to overcome wrong attitudes because what is often at stake is not just you and your future, but the future of your children and those closest to you. Many times our children do not have a better way to relate to successful living than to use their parents' lives as the model by which they measure success. The bottom line is that our attitudes and actions continue to impact lives in future generations. The desire to bear long-term fruit should motivate us to steward well the seeds we sow today.

A man with an unusual plan in Abilene, Texas, recently entered a *Chick-fil-A* and approached the counter with a grin. He gave the young cashier one thousand dollars with this instruction: "Use this cash to pay for all the drive-through orders until it's all gone." It was a Monday and the generous man wanted as many people as possible to have a good day. His gift gave nearly one hundred carloads of customers a free lunch. This unmerited kindness from a stranger brought one commuter to tears because her Monday morning had been particularly awful.

In Redding, California, an employee at a well-known coffee establishment witnessed four continuous hours of drive-thru customers paying for the coffee orders of the stranger behind them in line.

One particular community has several citizens who delight in finding someone unassuming in a restaurant and pay for their meal without their knowledge.

A man in the Carolinas found a way to put a new pair of shoes on children in his region who had never experienced such customized footwear.

Whether you have a large gift to give or you have just enough to share with the person in line behind you, give yourself away. Gifts given in secret are selfless and gratifying. Creative giving will soon be an ingrained habit as you become addicted to looking for others to bless.

My elderly parents live generous lives. Even in the midst of aging and diminished health my parents look for ways to bless others. One kind deed they do weekly has now become competitive. Dad waits till the garbage man empties the neighbor's trash, then he promptly takes the empty garbage cans back to the neighbor's house. It didn't take long for their neighbor to identify Dad as the helpful neighbor. One day Dad saw his neighbor pulling out of his driveway as the garbage man finished with their street. But Dad's neighbor saw his opportunity to beat my Dad's efforts in his rear view mirror. He put his truck in reverse and sped back to their adjoining driveways. Dad's neighbor managed to win the kindness award that day by reaching the empty garbage cans first, and placed my parents' cans back near their garage before Dad had time to even open the front door.

Most never take the time to even notice the needs of another, let alone compete to be the first to bless them. When you learn how to give yourself away in good deeds, encouragement, and alertness to the needs and desires of others, even seasons of transition will not be self-consuming. You will live life with a higher level of satisfaction. What once took conscious effort quickly becomes a way of life.

Recently I visited with one of my favorite groups of musical colleagues, the Perkins Family. We first met when we worked together for the same organization. It was love at first sight. The Perkins family loves, laughs, and cares for people in wild, and sometimes crazy, ways. They play good-natured pranks on those they love and keep them guessing what will be next.

Dale is the patriarch and chief instigator of these shenanigans. For years I have had a two-minute radio feature heard weekdays across the nation. But Dale likes me to do a customized one, on demand, every time I see him. He typically picks the subject matter or the person who will be the central focus of my commentary. With a big laugh and an arm around my shoulder, he turns in my direction and says, "Go." And it is my joy to accommodate his request. One time while we were together in Arkansas, Dale and their group of twenty or more, circled around me with video cameras in-hand, ready to shoot live footage. With no warning, Dale asked me to produce a customized feature for his granddaughter, Alese, who would be married in a few short weeks. Alese is my sweet friend, too, and I am thankful I think fast on my feet.

Later I received a text from Dale, telling me the video shot that day of my two-minute personal encouragement will be part of a visual presentation for Alese at her wedding. A simple, seemingly insignificant, action in one day is monumental on another. In all honesty, it only takes the slightest effort to go the extra mile.

There are many ways your giving can take shape. Here are a few examples of how one individual gave to another with no conditions or expectations:

A man stood in the grocery line with a few items. While waiting for those ahead of him to complete their transactions, he noticed the frazzled young mother behind him. She had a cart full of groceries and two little ones in tow. Suddenly he had a creative idea. Leaning in close to the cashier as his order was tallied, the man quickly instructed the cashier to credit his card for an additional hundred dollars. He wanted the amount to be applied to the young mother's grocery order. He then instructed that whatever is left over to give to the mother in cash.

During the busy holidays, a pastor surprised the waitress of his favorite restaurant with a large tip. The server burst into tears when she saw the generous tip he gave her. She gushed, saying, "I am a single mother and had no money for Christmas for my little girl. Thank you so much."

A special couple wrote us to announce they were getting a new truck and wanted to give us their old one. What a great surprise! That three-year-old SUV was perfect for an immediate need we had, and it is a joy to drive.

What might you accomplish if *stuck* were removed from your vocabulary and from your attitude? Aspire to a new level of generosity and thoughtful living. It is great fun to treat people as the treasures they truly are. An intentional transition into a person of generosity transforms you into a completely different person.

I have heard it said by others that they do not "give to get." However, the natural and inevitable process of sowing seed places you in the category of increase, like it or not. Though I agree, our attitude of giving should be pure and not selfishly opportunistic, there is something denied in the statement that we should not "give to get." Such an attitude is counterintuitive to the very nature of seeds. Ask any grain farmer if advocating such a philosophy makes sense. The fact is seeds are undeniably *designed* to reproduce. And seeds reproduce exponentially, so there is both a harvest we can all enjoy and much left over to plant again in another season.

I love the ancient passage that states, "Keep sowing your seed for you don't know which will grow—perhaps it all will."

Keep sowing your seed. Live to give, go to sow, and reap the exponential potential of making a difference in the lives of others with your random acts of kindness. You're not stuck—you've been positioned.

PASSION

Air travel is a large part of my busy life as a speaker so I look forward to meeting the person seated beside me. Long before *Stuck or Positioned* was the title of this book, I used this prepositional notion as an icebreaker in conversations with those I met in my travels. Engaging others in this unusual topic of conversation usually prompts a beautiful and memorable interchange. And then there are those conversations that are only memorable.

On my flight it seemed the seat beside me would not be filled. Then, at the last possible moment, a gentleman rushed passed the greeting attendant, pushed his way down the aisle and took the seat next to mine. He appeared frazzled. I waited until he got settled. After the flight attendants gave the safety review and the directive to have all electronic items put away, I pondered if I even wanted to start a conversation with my new travel mate. As soon as I tried to engage him in friendly conversation he revealed his impaired attitude. After the ascent, I began my favorite line of questioning.

"Are you headed home today or on your way to work?"

"Work."

"What do you do?" I asked.

"Sell lights."

"What kind of lights?"

This time he mumbled, "Large lights," but did not even turn to acknowledge me.

"Where do you put these lights?"

He robotically said, "Stadiums."

My chances of a lengthy conversation were slim but still, I was curious enough to continue, "Do you *like* what you do?"

He emphatically said, "Not at all."

I half-wondered if I should just bag this conversation and look for my headphones instead. But I really wanted to finish my survey. So, I took a deep breath and pressed on with my follow up questions.

"What is your passion?"

He stared straight ahead at the back of the seat in front of him as he glibly conceded, "I have no idea."

I was convinced he just did not want to talk. But because I am acutely aware everyone is in need of encouragement, I bravely asked one final question. "Sir, if you did know your passion, *and* if you could be paid to do it, would you pursue it?"

He became suddenly animated. He quickly snapped his face in my direction and then half-snarling said, "Lady, are you crazy? I have two kids to raise. That would be too risky."

Finally, I reached for the headphones in my purse.

My fellow passenger represents a majority of people who believe it is too risky to live their passion. Where did this prevailing notion come from? Most have convinced themselves they can't live their passion so why identify it? Again, I wonder where they got such a thought. One of my husband's favorite quotes from Michel de Montaigne is, "No wind serves him who addresses his voyage to no certain port." Identifying your passion is key to moving from a feeling of stuck to the reassuring knowledge that you are strategically positioned for the next great chapter of your life.

During a speaking tour on the east coast, I was interviewed on a global television-show. While we were there, I had the chance to meet a movie executive. As we got to know each other, he likened my life and work to a battleship. The point of his theme was well taken. I had known some real battles on life's ocean, not the least of which was the fight for my children and consequently losing my eyesight. This alone created a layer of struggle and hardship in my marriage and family. Battles and setbacks had at times left me worn and weary.

But then he used the metaphor to make a different point. He said, "Having a battleship in dry dock for a season is not unusual. I perceive you may be there now."

Battles, yes. Dry dock? That was not something I readily accepted. After all, wasn't I in the middle of releasing a new book? Wasn't public interest in my story mounting, and my speaking career growing? It sobered me to be sure. And honestly, because of his probing insights, I started to think deeply about my life and its mission like never before.

I was not sure I wanted to risk what it would take to end up on the front lines of any battle. I tried to dismiss it all when we left. The whole experience shook me in my innermost parts. I knew our lives were dedicated to more than just the normal cycle of life. And now I asked myself, "But at what cost? What could it all mean?" I pondered over these questions as we headed to the airport.

The clarification necessary to proceed on our life's journey sometimes comes from the most unlikely sources. Mine came later that very day from our chauffeur as he drove us to the airport. Because we were surrounded by a strong military culture throughout our stay in Virginia Beach, and based on our driver's age, I took a guess at his former career.

"Are you retired from the military?"

"Yes. How did you know?"

I confessed that I speculated and I thanked him for his service. He was truly appreciative. Then I asked, "What branch of the military did you choose for your career?"

"The Navy," he answered with pride.

I told him my father was also a Navy man who fought in the Korean War. I continued to ask more questions about his life before striking a gold mine. "What was your specific job in the Navy?"

He replied, "I took care of battleships."

Waves of chills swept up and down my spine. "Sir, could you please tell me what happens when a battleship is brought into dry dock?"

"Usually battleships are brought in so we can refurbish them. We update them to modern standards, and then they're sent out again."

"What does that entail exactly?"

"With an older battleship, instead of using regular fuel, we retrofit it to run on nuclear power. It will run for nearly thirty-five years before it needs refueling," he explained.

I sat back in silence pondering all I had just learned. I recognized that dry dock is not a place of punishment or abandonment, which I assumed, but simply a place of renewal. I could rest in the reassurance that I would not be stuck there. From the position of dry dock and its safe harbor, I would be empowered to go further and accomplish more. I had always been diligent in my pursuit of my dreams and desires. Yet, suddenly I wondered, were my dreams big enough?

Between the words of the film executive and those of the chauffeur I obtained a firmer grip on the realities of my life's mission. There are times I am stuck temporarily only to find new energy from a retrofit. It makes me a better person and better equips me to serve the people in my sphere of influence. I am not sure how many years of "fuel" I have left, but this much I know is true: I have today and, no matter the challenges I face, I believe I am empowered with purpose and vision.

Where do you begin to locate your passion? Look at the example below of a conversation I had with a friend who was trying to discover his passion. If you and I sat together over coffee, I would ask you a similar series of questions.

"Do you like what you do?"

He answered, "Well, I'm good at it. I've done it for twenty-two years. My wife and I own this business."

"But do you love what you do?"

He replied, "No, not really. I actually love finance." He told me that for years he has studied finance on his own time, and is an avid reader of anything in the financial world. "It's the first thing on my mind when I wake up in the morning. I think about it all day long. And it's the last thing on my mind before I go to bed at night."

I said, "Work your passion. What keeps you from being in finance?"

He paused, "I would have to expand my degree and get licensed."

"Then do it. Live your passion. It's not too late."

He laughed and said, "I'm really excited. I will do it."

After some more talk and encouragement, he startled me when he smacked the tabletop between us and said, "In thirty minutes you have completely changed my life."

I smiled, "I'm going to hold you accountable to follow your passion."

He enthusiastically answered, "When we talk next I will know the exact steps I need to take."

Your passion has value. Let me help you dismantle your fears by challenging you to look at your life from a fresh vantage point. Look for opportunities to turn mountains of difficulties into small bumps in the road. Keep your focus on what you currently have on hand. Resist the urge to be distracted by what you lack.

I am a national speaker and love what I get to do. It creates opportunities to deliver passion. I hold my profession in high esteem. I am constantly editing, changing, and expanding, sometimes while I am actually speaking. After all, I don't use notes. In the final analysis I apply the art of capturing my audience and knowing exactly where I want to take them. I work to have their best interest in mind. It is in my DNA to cast vision and lift the spirits of people. My personal measurement for success is transformed lives.

Perhaps your dream looks like everyone else's dream. It seems common. Just the fact it is a dream makes it special. You can add value by customizing it to showcase your passion and skills. Work and study to master your passion. Excel. Make new molds and raise the bar for new goals and standards. There is plenty of room for you to live your passion.

If you are in the season of dry dock, don't let it discourage you. Remember you're not stuck. A retrofit is underway. At dry dock you are retooled for a purposeful future as your passions are refueled. I remind you, "Your gift will make a way for you." Some barnacles may need to be removed to help speed up your course. And, the new paint job will highlight the new you.

Take the time to rediscover your life's passion. In doing so, I am convinced you will find a new source of energy and a rejuvenated heart. A vast ocean of possibilities awaits you. Get ready to launch. Then, full steam ahead. You're not stuck—you've been positioned.

BEYOND

Some people think they're stuck because they're faced with limited options. How shortsighted! When I think of my friend Martin, I know that anything is possible. Raised among the beautiful bluegrass of Kentucky, he was one of ten children. He loved business—he was a natural. His early success started in eighth grade. One day his father announced an offer to his sons. "Boys, I have a piece of land, if you want to grow something."

Martin jumped at the opportunity. He chose watermelons for his first crop, and with seeds and shovel in hand he quickly developed a strategy. Martin found a blue ribbon recipe for growing a bountiful crop. His secret consisted of removing two scoops of dirt and replacing them with two scoops of manure. He then covered the manure with the two scoops of dirt he originally took out. In each mound of earthy ingredients he planted eight watermelon seeds. His football-field size plot turned into a goldmine by the end of summer. When most young boys were playing games on the surface of the soil, Martin was digging for unseen potential.

After a fertile season and a bumper crop, Martin sold more than one thousand watermelons to passing motorists vacationing at the Kentucky lakes. By the end of the first summer, Martin had thousands of dollars in a cigar box, which he used as his makeshift bank.

This endeavor was only the beginning of fertile fields, innovative enterprise, and determined vision.

While growing up, Martin and his siblings were encouraged and expected to work on the family farm. However, Martin was given permission to help a neighbor run his gas station, which, in time, proved to be providential. His junior year of high school his father took a huge risk and invested his entire savings into a full service mechanic and gas station. After high school Martin exchanged his all-star basketball skills to focus solely on a college business degree while working in the service station and on the farm.

In his freshman year of college, Martin had an idea for a joint business venture with his father. He had learned that a Five Star Food Mart chain of convenience stores with gasoline pumps was being introduced to Kentucky. Martin marveled when his father agreed to trust the businessman his son had become, even at a young age. They converted the gasoline service station into a convenience store. No more grease monkey! It was a success. The result of their efforts provided enough income to pay for Martin's education, for his father's retirement, and later, funding when his mother was widowed.

Personal success is frequently tried in the adversity of dark times, and Martin's success was no exception. When Martin was a young adult with a young wife and a new baby, he discovered his business partner had embezzled money and hid their equipment. Martin was left holding the bank note and had plenty of reasons for bitterness to take over. Instead, he recovered, and rebuilt his business. In time, he was a competitor to the man who first betrayed him, and the tables turned. Each step along the way, including his setbacks and business challenges, prepared Martin for his current success. He now owns and oversees multiple businesses. The old adage about "you can take the boy out of the country but not the country out of the boy" is true with Martin. A tractor is still his love and the farm roots of his success have grown from that first patch of possibilities.

The thing I love about Martin is that he isn't wrapped up in his own prideful world of success. Martin's personal enterprises continue to flourish; yet he makes time to mentor other young business-minded people. You can do the same. Don't envy the success of others, but *learn* from their example and choose to grow. Martin remains outstanding in his field, even today. You may hear Martin's story and think he was destined for greatness. Think again. His dreams, like yours, had interruptions, setbacks, and hard times. It's life. Why does it catch you off guard?

When people talk about life's disappointments and failed dreams, the phrase "crash and burn" is often mentioned. But what folks fail to realize is that in the midst of a disaster is the power to focus on the positive. Are you focused merely on enduring life's calamities or on being grateful for what you walked away with—your life? You're not dead if you are still breathing. See your life's story for what it is: epic and evolving.

Recently, I called my friend, William, and asked him to recount for me his own survival story. In July of 1990 William drove from Brunswick, Georgia, to Spartanburg, South Carolina, to speak at the first session of a father-son seminar. William's father, the other part of the speaking team, could not come until later in the day and did so via a flight provided by a family friend and pilot. William's demanding schedule as a lawyer and judge required him to leave before the seminar ended. He took his father's seat and would return on the same airplane.

William boarded the Cessna 340 for the flight to the Golden Isles of Georgia. The pilot informed him they would first make a quick stop in Atlanta to pick up one more passenger.

Upon their approach to Charlie Brown Airport in Fulton County both engines stopped. Without warning, the Cessna careened into a steep descent. The pilot worked feverishly to re-start the engines while shouting in his headset, "*May Day! May Day!*" William, seated in the co-pilot's seat, watched their free fall out the windshield with the terrifying view of the inevitable. He wondered if this would be the end of his life.

They were headed for a grove of trees, their only hope of cushioning their crash. The impact was harsh, with the tree branches perforating the fuselage, especially on the pilot's side. The plane pancaked between trees and landed nose down. Branches, broken glass, and jagged sheet metal shot into the cockpit like shrapnel. The largest tree limb erupted through the floor between William and the pilot. Thankfully, their plane was spindled to a halt. Both men were knocked unconscious when they were thrown into the control panel. William recalled feeling a hand patting his face and hearing a voice instructing him to quickly wake up. William tried to move but could not lift his finger. He feared his neck was broken. Gradually he felt the energy returning to his body. Then he looked at the burly pilot slumped unconscious over the yoke. He was aware of the smell of fuel. Fearing that they might be consumed in a ball of fire, William found a surge of strength not present moments earlier.

William rose up and moved towards the rear of the interior, climbing up and over a tangle of tree branches and jagged wreckage. He located the rear door and struggled to open it. With the escape door open, William stretched downward to leverage the bleeding pilot out of his seat, but couldn't reach him. He jerked out a seat bolted in the aluminum frame to get behind the pilot. Still unable to move or unbuckle him, William once more yanked a second bolted seat from the plane. Now that he was more favorably positioned, he wrangled the pilot up toward the plane's rear door and eventually freed him from the wreckage. By that time the pilot was regaining consciousness.

The stench of fuel grew steadily stronger as William walked the pilot as far from the craft as possible. At about one hundred feet from the crash site, the pilot collapsed under the shade of a tree. With the sound of sirens drawing steadily nearer, William realized he must overcome yet another obstacle in order to be rescued. The wreckage wasn't visible from the highway, so the first responders could lose precious time hunting for survivors. He walked through the thick woods towards the sound of the sirens and finally flagged down the emergency crew to direct them to the injured man.

Paramedics scrambled to get both men ready for the hospital transport. When my friend learned that a helicopter was on its way to pick them up, William flat-out refused the offer, as he firmly said, "I am not flying on anything else today!"

Perhaps, the reason we feel stuck in life is that we try to match the task in front of us with our own ability and strength. Our vision is not fully fixed on the possibilities. William's reach was limited but his experiences were evidence that his mother's prayers were heard that day. Unbeknownst to anyone else, she took a moment before the plane left Georgia initially to purposefully pray a blessing of protection over the aircraft that would carry special cargo dear to her heart. The audible warning William heard; his inordinate physical strength; his clarity of mind; and his selfless action to care for another all highlight the intersection where his abilities ended and divine intervention took over.

Prayer is never a crutch but a bridge, an extension from the place where you presently feel stuck to the position intended for you. William is a case in point. His leadership skills continue to help others. His work as a state legislator embodies noble service as he extends himself on behalf of the people he serves.

Perhaps the plane crash worked to refocus William's life purpose so he could be better used in his role in the Georgia State Senate. There, he is strategically positioned to impact his culture.

I love the word *beyond*, especially when I feel stuck. It denotes a place I've never been; a place I've never seen; a frontier of new discovery. Yet, I still wonder why people live life based only on what they see, contented with their status quo.

Farris walked with his ranch manager through the rigid terrain of his ranch. His manager knew the land well and pointed out places of interest to the new owner. In passing, the manager told of a raging brook that once flowed through this current dry spot. The spring water halted because of shifting underground rock that now blocked the flow.

Farris, a man of faith, simply prayed in a conversational way and asked for something beyond his own ability. He addressed God by his name, saying, as he walked the land, "Yahweh, it would be great if you would restore that river." His personal walk of faith did not need any pulpit or ceremony. Farris simply requested an answer beyond his reach.

Months passed.

Later, Farris returned to the ranch for a visit. His ranch manager realized he had forgotten to tell Farris what happened after he first prayed so many months ago. Where a dry bed had previously existed now a bubbling brook flowed freely. I personally heard the video the day they discovered the divine surprise.

Do you have a dried up spring within your soul? Ask for the living spring to bubble up and overflow again in your life and rejoice. A simple conversation just might do it. Nothing is impossible.

David is a bilingual young American from our area of Dallas, but I had to travel halfway around the world in order to meet him. We first met in Spain while I was on a speaking tour. David worked there as an intern. When I first heard him speak I thought he might be battling laryngitis because David only whispered.

Instead of having his voice crack and change as an adolescent, David completely lost his voice. In fact, David was a medical mystery. At first, everyone thought his voice would come back in time. Some doctors were convinced it was a psychosomatic way to get more attention. But, after many doctor exams and tests, a specialist confirmed the change in this young man's soft voice was permanent. David's vocal cords were paralyzed. Physicians consider his condition irreversible and non-operable. He was labeled, "beyond help."

I asked David to identify his greatest challenges. He told me, "The most frustrating part isn't the confused faces when I talk, or the snickering when I introduced myself to someone new. The most frustrating part was when I knew I wasn't going to sing anymore. That hit home the hardest."

David continued, "Of course there were the little things I had to give up along the way, like ordering fast food at the drive-thru, carrying on dinner conversations in a loud room, and talking on the phone. In the beginning, it was beyond overwhelming. As I faced my limitations and loss, the greatest temptations were seething anger and bitterness. I was angry with those who tried to diagnose my condition, angry at God for allowing it, and angry at myself for wondering if I had done something to deserve it. But I got sick of being angry and bitter real fast."

You see, David came to the conclusion that bitter people are among some of the most unattractive people in the world, "And I didn't want to be that. I still knew one thing; I knew God had something special for my life."

I asked David what counsel helped him most in his loss. "Some of the best advice I have ever received from a mentor is this. For things to change you have to change. And for things to get better you have to get better. As you change, everything will change for you. It doesn't mean you control God's timing. But, it does mean you can change your mind, your attitude, and how you look at what some people call a disability. You can use what was meant for harm. My simple prayer was, 'God, I don't know what you're doing, but whatever it is you want me to do, the answer is "Yes." I just want you to use me.' And that simple prayer has changed my perspective on what I carry."

David and I have worked together on many projects since we first met. It's odd that David is unable to speak and I am unable to see. It may look like a double disadvantage. However, we work circles around most, and together we have collaborated to produce many video presentations.

We both love witty humor and dislike whiners because we know they could be winners, if only they would try. The humor has nothing to do with our loss but, instead, our shared victories in spite of loss. We often banter back and forth with amiable humor reserved only for those in the middle of a challenge. David frequently asks me to "look at his finished video projects" and I tell him to "keep his voice down."

Neither of us is beyond help or hope. David's musicianship, communication skills and creativity are priceless gems, but his overcoming spirit is pure gold. David is a champion whose very life eagerly exhibits to those in circumstances beyond their control, "You're not stuck!"

Reach beyond yourself and find new dimensions of hope, purpose, and joy. There is more. You're not stuck—you've been positioned.

CHOICES

Our lives consist of a series of choices. And those choices all have consequences. Some consequences are immediately realized and only affect you. Yet, equally significant consequences can impact the next generation. Understanding the snowball effect of decision-making is key for sound decisions. As you continue to chart your life's course, I have an important question for you to consider: What is your core compass?

It's unfortunate the abiding legacy of President Richard Nixon's tenure in office is his political suicide and resignation, for there are important lessons we can learn from a less well-known decision he made during that tumultuous time. It was during the darkest period of his presidency and at the point of his lowest popularity ratings when President Nixon did something that remains significant to this day: he helped save a nation.

On October 6, 1973, the Yom Kippur War broke out in Israel and their odds of survival as a nation and as a people were slim, indeed. At a critical juncture, Prime Minister Golda Meir called President Nixon in the middle of the night, desperate for help. The war had exhausted Israel's weaponry and threatened the nation's security and very existence. The free world has always stood in amazement of Israel, the lone democracy in the Middle East, surrounded by vastly populated enemy nations, yet only the size of New Jersey.

When our unpopular president heard the voice of Prime Minister Meir on the other end of the phone, he simultaneously heard the voice of the most influential person in his life. Nixon's mother had told him years earlier that one day he would be in a powerful position to help the Jewish people. Her devout faith as a Quaker acted as a compass in her son's formative years, long before he became the president of the United States. Though in crisis himself, Nixon acted swiftly. Anything Israel needed was immediately sent. In twenty-four hours the requested emergency help and supplies were in the hands of the Israelis. Prime Minister Meir referred to Richard Nixon as "my President." Golda's glowing praise for her American ally continued, "For generations to come, all will be told of the miracle of the immense planes from the United States bringing in the material that meant life to our people." Consequently, President Nixon is highly respected in that small nation to this day.

What if he had not taken the Prime Minister's call that night? What if he had not heeded the prophetic counsel of his mother? More is at stake than we may realize when we are faced with life's choices. My own father often told me, "You can have anything you want, but you must choose wisely." The sobering fact remains. Our choices impact others beyond anything we can presently see.

Rosa Parks changed history by a simple decision she made in 1955 during the mounting racial unrest in our nation. In her hometown of Montgomery, Alabama, Rosa refused to give her seat on the bus to a white man. Her simple and steadfast choice was a history maker. Her choice was not prodded by television cameras, or coaxed by organized protests, or coerced through megaphones. Rosa Parks simply said, with her body language and a simple choice, "Enough!" Her action resisted the popular prejudice of segregation.

Rosa's courageous and daring choice brought international attention to the injustice of one ethnic group weary of their assigned seats in the back of the bus.

On the very day Rosa was convicted of violating the segregation laws of her state, an organized bus boycott began. Leading a peaceful protest was a young preacher named Dr. Martin Luther King Jr. Through Dr. King's skillful leadership, local black community leaders continued to organize. More than one year later, Rosa Parks' controversial struggle for equality ended with the U.S. Supreme Court ruling bus segregation as unconstitutional. Consequently, Rosa Parks became the national symbol of dignity and strength. When Rosa peacefully *chose* to remain seated on that bus, doors of opportunity opened for generations yet to come.

As a child, I often heard the story of a simple choice my parents made that changed the course of their lives forever. After their honeymoon in the panhandle of Florida, they returned to their apartment in St. Louis where Dad was enrolled at a university on his G.I. Bill, awarded for his faithful years of service in the U.S. Navy during the Korean War. Classes were to start in the fall. After the landlady gave them the keys, she told them they had received a letter. Without unpacking their car, they went upstairs to their little one-room efficiency to read the letter. It was a request for them to help a small congregation in south Missouri through the summer. They returned the apartment keys, left the car packed, and headed for an unfamiliar destination halfway across the state. That one crucial decision laid the foundation for their young lives, a foundation on which all subsequent decisions would come to rest.

This unsolicited request included Dad's overseeing and preaching at this church, as well as other nearby churches, for the four years he was in college. Looking back, it was in that defining moment that led my parents to decide to invest their lives in service to others. They accepted the immediate negative consequence of losing their deposit on that first apartment and moved to Rolla, Missouri, where he enrolled in one of the top engineering schools in the United States. They've never regretted taking that leap of faith and neither have the Missouri townspeople of Salem, Goodwater, and Jadwin, who benefitted from four years of my parents' loving leadership.

I had to make a choice one day without any forewarning or preparation. I underwent a series of eye tests due to a small broken vessel seen in my last eye exam. After four hours of thorough and intense exams, I was told I had to choose that day between the baby I carried in my womb and my eyes. I did not take time to think over my decision. It was crystal clear to me in that moment. "I choose my baby." My doctor stood up and slammed my folder shut as he said, "What a foolish decision," and left the room.

I knew life was a gift. I sat alone with my head spinning but my heart anchored. Candidly, I did not know all the challenges or the ramifications for my future, yet I knew choosing life over death was the right choice. I am asked frequently, "Why did you do it?" I struggle to answer their questions with an answer that puts them at peace and describes my quick response. I wonder if the core of the *real* question is, "How did you choose between convenience and legacy?"

In my life, legacy wins hands down every time. My life has been full and my husband and I enjoy five children the doctors said we would never have. My eyesight gradually diminished having the children. Though I long to see, I see more than most give me credit. I see opportunities. I see potential. I see destiny. I practice seeing and I watch for opportunities and life lessons most visual types overlook. I focus on people, and my perspective on life has inspired multiple thousands. My choice now is to live with vision, even though my eyesight is beyond medical help.

The child I carried in my womb the day of the doctor's visit is our second-born daughter. She is our first married child, and she gave us our first grandchildren. Looking back on that fateful day, I find a high sense of purpose in the choice I made. My vision for the lives of all my children is that their achievements in life exceed my own. I hope to be a set of solid shoulders for the next generation to stand on to successfully influence their generation. The results of wise choices made by one generation won't be fully tallied until that generation has passed. Think about your own life and the decisions you've made. Follow the thread of consequences and ramifications. For some this may be painful, but you still have today to choose life and to choose wisely.

John was an Army Sergeant who served our country in both Iraq and Afghanistan. His dangerous assignment was to lead his team in detecting and destroying Improvised Explosive Devices (IED) planted by the enemy. John performed his leadership duties while seated in a specialized rig called the "Buffalo." This six-wheel, thirty-ton vehicle used a twenty-foot hydraulic arm to reach buried explosives and either detonate them, or hand them over to bomb technicians.

Near the end of one particularly exhausting night, John and his team headed back to the base. Two miles out, John noticed the checkpoint they were approaching was unmanned. Slowing their vehicle, they watched two other vehicles cautiously pass through the area without incident. But when John's vehicle entered the suspicious area, an IED exploded with a straight hit to the side of their rig.

John was briefly knocked unconscious but quickly awakened with the sound of blood curdling screams from the soldier behind him. In the darkened cab John groped for a flashlight. The beam of light revealed the extent of his buddy's injuries: both of the soldier's legs had been blown off in the blast. John shouted for the driver, still recovering from the shock of the blast, to hand him his Army-issued tourniquet. Pulling his own tourniquet from the pocket of his uniform, John applied one to each of what remained of the soldier's legs. As gruesome as that scene was, John said he knew he had to get back where his friend was lying in the middle aisle. He chose to keep going. John says, "I didn't want someone else to come into the vehicle. I decided I must help."

Nate, the gravely wounded warrior, was air lifted to safety and survived. As a double amputee, he now has many incredible achievements in Iron Man competitions and in hand-bike racing.

John's valiant actions and service to our country were the result of a series of noble, intentional choices he made. John and countless brave men and women in our military are worthy of heartfelt honor. I initially interviewed John on an anniversary eve of September 11th. After thanking him for his military service, I asked what he was thinking. He pointed out the September 11, 2001, attack is what motivated him to enlist in the military and eventually serve in Iraq. John said, "I have been so proud to serve and my little bit of pain is nothing compared to what thousands of our military have dealt with. Tomorrow (September 11th) is the day I want to be with the guys."

John's selfless efforts have resulted in visible scars and daily pain. He remembers yesterday but chooses to forgive and move on. This team leader chose to exhibit extraordinary courage in the face of war. We can all deliberately choose to put the needs of others before our own. All of us can live with them in mind.

A pastor once counseled a troubled young man named Ben. This newly married man was plagued with fears of ruining his marriage. The bridegroom confessed he feared being abusive like his father. While Ben continued speaking, the pastor took out a blank sheet of paper and quickly wrote on it. Then he interrupted Ben's fretting by sliding the paper in front of the anxious young man.

Picking up the paper, Ben quickly noticed a makeshift permission slip scrawled in the pastor's rough handwriting. The document began, "I, Ben's father…" At the side of this statement the pastor asked for and actually printed the full name of Ben's father. Then the text continued, "I, Ben's father, give my son, Ben, full permission in his generation to abuse his wife and the mother of his children like I did in my generation. Ben is hereby authorized, by the model I left him and by any means possible, to abuse as he sees fit."

The pastor's efforts to get Ben's attention were now obvious. The balance of the document included the signature of Ben's father, provided in proxy by the pastor, and the date. Shocked by the permission slip, Ben looked sternly at the pastor. This did not address his fear, it only increased it. "Pastor, what is this about?"

The pastor explained, "Like it or not, the most authoritative person in your life is your father. Whether you loved him or hated him, you are drawn to your father's model, otherwise you would not be here in my office. Your father established a standard you are wise enough to know is not the kind of standard you want for your life. But until you decide that his model is not going to be yours, you are likely to project your father's model onto yourself by the sheer emotional connection you have with him. Until you make a calculated personal decision to do what you must with that permission slip, you could repeat the history you so despise and fear. You don't have to dishonor your dad, because he will always be your father, but what you do with that permission slip will determine your future."

Ben ripped up the permission slip without a moment's hesitation. This formerly troubled man walked free of his fear. He was given the choice to live differently, and he walked out of that office a free man.

Take time to reflect on how you now live based on how those before you lived. Have you been stuck following the mired footprints of former generations? New choices, based on principled living, can create a new future for you. How will you script your permission slip for the next generation?

My friend, Bob, a former congressman, was active in bringing about the collapse of the Soviet Union. Bob knows firsthand the fruits of freedom. He believes there are only two main choices in life, two worldviews, which determine every subsequent decision. Bob contends, "Either you believe that God made man, or you believe that man made God." Depending on which belief system you choose, every decision going forward will be built on the premise of that choice."

If man made God then it is easy to ignore Him and live life apart from the way of divine wisdom and counsel. It is also easy to carve out the god you want to embrace and make up your own rules. It eliminates the annoying notions of absolutes, consequences, accountability and guidelines. With this choice you won't need a moral code or a compass, as man is in charge of his own destiny.

However, if God created man then the choice to honor His ways and live according to His wise counsel is imperative. There is no middle ground. Carefully weigh the decisions in your life. Your choices will influence more than you can now see.

In a day of assorted choices you *can* access the greater wisdom that anchors you for better days ahead. You're not stuck—you've been positioned.

STALL

One afternoon my husband dropped our family off to go ice skating at the downtown civic center. We lived in Central Illinois at the time, and a close group of young mothers often coordinated special outings with all our children.

As the afternoon progressed, none of us realized just how long my husband Tony had been gone. Imagine our shock hours later to see him pull up to the entrance of the civic center with our van covered in feathers and half of the windshield caved in! A small crowd gathered to examine the damage and question my husband.

"What on earth happened?" I gasped. Tony explained he had been running errands on the east side of town while we enjoyed our skating. On his way back, he had a surprise collision. A large goose was waddling down the middle of the two-lane highway. He saw the creature from several hundred yards away, but didn't worry because he saw the bird begin to lift-off. He fully expected the goose to become airborne in plenty of time. Tony slowed as it became increasingly obvious that this lumbering bird wasn't getting the needed lift. This goose was not only short on lift but also headed directly at his van. Tony braked and turned into the other lane to avoid an accident, but it was too late. The bird's weight, combined with its tardy takeoff and its choice of a busy highway "runway," led to the fowl's untimely demise.

Just as the graceless goose reached the point of no return, Tony only had time to shout, "You dumb bird!" before the goose crashed into the windshield in midflight. The passenger side of the windshield was shattered and feathers were everywhere. Even though the van was a mess, he knew we didn't have another way home, so here he was, now drawing a crowd of curious moms and kids. Even the antenna was covered in down. Our family van was a fine-feathered mess.

Later that evening, a local radio commentator reported that a lone goose had lost his companion on the east side of town. Half chuckling to myself about an obviously slow news day, it occurred to me the goose lost his life because he could not get his proper lift. It reminds me of many people I know who can never seem to get the lead out. They are often weighed down by cares and fears instead of preparing intentionally to take on life's risks. Too late in life they try to position their dreams for takeoff, only to discover they need a longer runway. It is not about lacking talent. It's about inaccurately estimating the cost and time to successfully get things off the ground. Wasted years, postponed personal development, a shallow work ethic, or skills dulled by non-use render many people ill-matched for opportunities that cycle through their lives. They willfully exchange their precious gift of time for the latest craze in pop-culture, watching television, playing computer games, or amusing themselves for mindless hours with various forms of media. Their time would have been better spent in tapping mentors and teachers and in reading books or trade magazines.

One morning as I prepared for an upcoming speaking engagement I was awakened by a resounding phrase. It came from deep within. It said, "Quit stalling your calling." I am a professional speaker but rarely look for rhyming lines or catchy phrases, and the word stalling was not common to my vocabulary.

As I thought about "stalling," I was reminded of the fantastic air shows where airplanes perform death-defying aerobatics, stunning their audiences with their ability to maneuver swiftly through the air. They also deliberately create scenarios where they can stall the plane's engine in order to travel at significantly reduced speeds without crashing. It's unnerving because this dramatically demonstrates a life or death scenario. In the midst of a stalled engine there is a small window of time between falling out of the sky, getting the engine started again, and finding the lift to recover; to soar to even greater heights.

How often have we done the same in life? It is easy to hold back in hesitation, letting others set the pace and determine the direction of our course. When organizations ask for volunteers many make excuses as a stall tactic, hoping others will fill in and take the responsibility. Younger family members often stall after finishing a family meal, silently wishing someone else will initiate the cleanup. The same is true in leadership roles. Passive followers usually wait for ambitious leaders to shoulder the initiative.

Every aspiring actor or actress who auditions for a role has an initial goal in mind: to make the callback list. The order in which names appear on that list often determines who might get the leading role and who will be assigned supporting roles. Once the call is closed that particular opportunity is lost. Sometimes alternate roles are immediately available, but the actors usually have to knock on lots of other doors for another chance.

On the stage of your life, you have the leading role. It's the role for which you are perfectly suited and skilled to play. Have you not heard that a call has gone out for you to rise to the occasion?

This is not a dress rehearsal. Life is the stage and its platform is a place to shine. You are perfect for each new act with all its changing scenes. Others are watching your life closely, like understudies, hoping to learn something about life based on your performance. If you've been chiding yourself over lost opportunities in your past, please don't hesitate—knock on the doors of life again! There is a vital part you must play. Why would you stall when such opportunities are at your disposal? You have been given a callback notice. Come back to life; live it big and live it full.

Many people miss their call as they bury themselves in the counterfeits of life. The false realities of substance abuse, misplaced priorities, overbooked lives, uncontrolled anger, and mismanaged living lead them to unhappiness. They try to play a role that was never intended for them. They preoccupy themselves with false promises, shallow friendships, and a life without principles.

What about you? Are you struggling to get your dreams off the ground? Do you sense you're headed for a stall? A hesitation to reach higher can mean missing a significant opportunity. It's understandable if along life's way you've developed a fear of failure. If you're like me, you may feel that trouble and misery have a knack for knocking on your door. Does insecurity frequently stalk you? Keep your focus. Step up and take your part in life's epic play. There is a call that has gone out and you are needed to play your part. No one else can fill the bill. Only you will do.

Many years ago, my uncle Carl took my Granny flying in his small airplane. For years, Granny had said she wanted to be one of the first grandmothers in the country to get her private pilot's license. She rode next to her son-in-law that day, anticipating a great view and seeking the thrill of adventure. My uncle considered paved runways and municipal airports optional features of the aviation experience. He was accustomed to helping himself to grass strips and open pastures for his arrivals and departures. Their initial takeoff lacked height. Granny held her breath as the little plane barely propelled over the fence of an adjoining field before dropping back to the ground. Uncle Carl tried again. The wind picked up a bit and they eventually achieved the speed and lift necessary to remain airborne.

Uncle Carl flew Granny all the way from Indiana to Southeast Missouri where he prepared to land in one of the fields on Granny's farm. His final approach demanded he skillfully maneuver around power lines during their descent. No one knows the full story of the flight that day, but suffice it to say that Granny never flew again. Nor did she ever speak again of her dream to have her own pilot's license. But her decision did not alter my uncle's sense of adventure. I can imagine his sweet laugh as he said, "What a ride!"

Are you waiting for a fresh wind to catch your wings and carry you closer to your desires and dreams? What if the winds are steadily blowing, but you still lack the speed and thrust necessary to propel you to your desired altitude? Perhaps it's a weight and balance problem due to the excess baggage you're attempting to take with you. Make the necessary adjustments and then let the laws of aerodynamics do their thing.

Wisdom states, "Be ready in all seasons." Is this possible? Any good leader knows there is always more to learn. Skills and talents can always be improved. Observe the great golf champions of our day who continue in lessons and coaching on the heels of winning a major tournament. Professional athletes take practice seriously. They turn routine and fundamentals into a professional lifestyle that result in record-breaking championships and big earnings.

I talk with many who have stalled dreams because they have been talked out of them. Their excuses are: "It is too late;" "I'm too old;" "I'm too young;" "It's too hard;" or "I could never achieve it anyway, so why try?" Those stall tactics only lead to lost altitude. Perhaps you have decided it will not matter what you do with your life, but have you considered the others you are taking down with you?

Your decision to commit, or not commit, your dreams to flight will impact those around you. Your stall tactics might delay others from reaching their destinations in a timely fashion. The audience of the life you live benefits from your showing up to play your part. Don't stall any longer. Reach again. Dream again. Hope again.

Be willing to soar into new orbits for your own benefit—and for everyone your life touches.

In 1947 a test pilot by the name of Chuck Yeager was the first to break the sound barrier. Not knowing what he would face that fateful day, he embraced his family the morning of his mission, perhaps wondering if he would ever see them again. Many had gotten close to it, but the shaking, rattling, and uncontrollable sensation sent pilots who dared to attempt it back to a safer speed. However, Captain Yeager was determined. He would not be stopped until he tried.

The morning mission was clear and calm sailing until he approached the ominous barrier. Suddenly a violent shaking of the fuselage caused chaotic readings on his instrument panel. Everything seemed out of control. With his own body shaking, he was not deterred. For several moments—it seemed like an eternity—his focus was tempted by an obvious distraction. Finally, he pushed safely through that invisible yet powerful, barrier, thrilled to find calm on the other side.

How often do we face some barrier and everything around us is shaken? The discomfort of uncertainty intensifies as we begin to press through the ominous barriers in our path. No one would disrespect us for backing off to find a safer place. But, what if we tried to go beyond the real and imagined barriers of our dreams?

The only thing I vividly remember from Mrs. Fryer's fifth grade class is a poem by Edgar Albert Guest we were required to memorize:

Somebody said that it couldn't be done,

But, he with a chuckle replied

That "maybe it couldn't," but he would be one

Who wouldn't say so till he'd tried.

So he buckled right in with the trace of a grin

On his face. If he worried he hid it.
He started to sing as he tackled the thing
That couldn't be done, and he did it.
Somebody scoffed: "Oh, you'll never do that;
At least no one has done it;"
But he took off his coat and he took off his hat,
And the first thing we knew he'd begun it.
With a lift of his chin and a bit of a grin,
Without any doubting or quiddit,
He started to sing as he tackled the thing
That couldn't be done, and he did it.
There are thousands to tell you it cannot be done,
There are thousands to prophesy failure;
There are thousands to point out to you one by one,
The dangers that wait to assail you.
But just buckle it in with a bit of a grin,
Just take off your coat and go to it;
Just start to sing as you tackle the thing
That "couldn't be done," and you'll do it.

Quit stalling. You are called to engage in living. The stage is set and you are specially chosen for your part. Take hold of it. Grow into it. It will soon be more than a mere performance, but a lifestyle and learning how to enjoy every moment of life. There are new frontiers to discover. Initiate, create, invent, and explore. You can engage in a life well lived. You're not stuck—you've been positioned.

MOVIE

One day my friend Dawn called and said she had a gift for me. Dawn is the kind of friend who is always thoughtful and generous. We inevitably make a memory somewhere and our outings always end in laughter. Dawn knows gifts are my love language and perfume is my absolute favorite. But today she had another idea. Instead she said, "I want to take you to the movies."

"The movies? Why would you take someone who cannot see to the movies and think that's a gift?" I literally moved the phone from my ear and looked skyward and said, "God, are these the only friends you could bring me?"

I put the phone back to my ear and listened as she continued to convince me, by saying, "Oh Gail, you'll love it! It's a movie filled with great dialogue about an elderly couple and their tender love." Finally convinced the time together would be fun, I said, "Sure, I'm game."

It would be a stretch to say the outing was a gift because I cried all the way through the film. It proved to be more than just another tender story. It touched a heartstring in me that made me weep. The movie mirrored my family's prolonged grief with Alzheimer's, which now held my mother-in-law in it's advanced stage. On a painfully personal level, the movie accentuated the cruelty of this dreaded disease.

The tender but grim tale finally ended, but my heartache was long from over. I wiped the tears from my eyes as I sat staring at the credits, though everything was a blur. The music cradled me while a million thoughts went through my mind.

Somewhat composed but still teary, I stood and made my way down the row of theater seats. Reaching for my friend, we silently walked up the aisle, arm in arm. When we reached the massive corridor, I stepped to the side for a moment to regain my composure, while Dawn excused herself to the ladies room.

I was grateful for a few minutes alone to finish processing all I had experienced. I needed to shift gears and prepare myself for the rest of the day. When you cannot see, you're not fully sure where you should stand. Though I could not see faces clearly, I sensed I was in the way of people moving back and forth in front of me. So I stepped back two big steps. Then, I moved to the right two more big steps to get completely out of the way. They just seemed like the right moves to make. I stood alone for quite some time wondering what was taking Dawn so long. It seemed like she should've been back for me by now.

Several more minutes passed and still my friend had not come to my rescue. Suddenly, I had a crazy thought. Why not greet people instead of looking like I'm lost? I'm not sure if it's because of my outgoing personality or the way I was raised, but when I'm around people, I try to engage them. A simple smile, a warm greeting, or casual conversation is my mode of operation. I love people, so I look for ways to encourage them. My only problem was not knowing exactly where to find them, even though I knew many were nearby.

"Hello!" I chirped, as I turned my head to the right, hoping I would gaze at someone passing in that direction. Undaunted, I continued, "Hi, how are you today?" I looked straight ahead to those I sensed were nearby. "Hey, how are you?" as I moved my head to the left to greet another person.

Still, no Dawn had come to retrieve me. But it really didn't matter because I was making the best of my situation. I was enjoying my position as the self-appointed greeter. I was ready to take on whatever the day would bring and make the most of it with a smile.

Finally, Dawn came back and I was shocked to hear alarm in her voice as she asked in a panic. "Gail, what are you *doing*? You're standing in the men's restroom!"

I often tell this story, and people try to comfort me later by saying, "Honey, I've walked into the wrong restroom before, too. Don't feel bad." However, I always want to exclaim, "Yes, but you didn't stand there greeting everyone!"

Perhaps I didn't know where I was supposed to be that day, and it may have looked like I was in the wrong place—stuck, but quite the contrary. On my way to where I should have been, I gave myself to the moment and to the people in that moment. I simply showed up and made a difference. I might have been in the wrong place, but I was all the way there.

Possibly you're standing at the wrong door today and wondering where you should be. Don't lose heart in the temporary mix-up of where you are and where you want to be. In time, you will find your way. You are not stuck; you've been positioned. Show up each day. Be all the way there. Make a difference.

Life is a journey. It takes twists and turns. Sometimes people live life thinking they only have one chance to find their way, and that's not true. Your journey sometimes feels like a marathon and at other times like a roller coaster ride. But each part of the journey has value. The journey is yours to oversee, but you never travel in isolation. On your journey your path will continually meet others and surprise appointments will develop.

Maximize the moment, even if you have to wait. Is it your physical location, or your attitude that defines whether you're stuck or positioned? Even if you're in the wrong place, it's usually embarrassingly temporary.

One of my favorite video clips on the Internet shows two people on a roller coaster at an amusement park. You don't know if you should laugh or cry when you see this clip because of the obvious pain of one and the elated joy of the other.

A woman and a young man are seated next to each other on the roller coaster. Their ride begins in typical fashion, with slow anticipation and a steady climb to the top. Then the excitement begins and they are jerked down the steepest of slopes. The woman's hands are raised in the air and her eyes wide open as she gives herself to the thrill of the moment. In sharp contrast, the young man is terrorized as he holds on with white knuckles and the look of horror on his face. The woman squeals with joy, and laughs exuberantly, while the young man screams for dear life, pleading for the ride to stop. As the video continues, the young man slips out of his seat into an unnatural position. His chin is caught on the security bar, which is the only thing that prevents him from flying out of the cart altogether.

The woman is enjoying the ride, but she is also aware of her companion. She can take in the excitement and take note of her young friend's anxiety. But the same is not true of the young man. He is totally engulfed in his own terrifying experience, and completely detached from anything outside that experience.

This view of life is common to mankind. Many love life and you can tell. They live life open-handed and happy. They enjoy every season of life with its twists and turns. Others hold on for dear life and wish it could be over, fearing what will come around the next curve. As a general rule, those who have decided to enjoy life are aware of the pain and struggle of others and are the most likely to offer a helping hand. Those whose perspective is just the opposite are far less likely to make a contribution to the culture around them. They are in survival mode. Both views of life, and all variations in between, have a common denominator—the ride.

Nic Vujicic is a marvel and his attitude convicting. Nic was born without arms and legs, but he knows how to live life with joy. He makes a difficulty look simple, and his willingness to try new things is beyond inspirational. He is courageous, yet tender. He gives his life to help others get the lead out of their feet and stop sitting on their hands. What makes the difference for him?

As a young child Nic experienced the startling reality of his physical limitations colliding with his dreams and aspirations. Born without arms and legs, he faced not just the normal challenges of school and adolescence, but he struggled with depression and thoughts of suicide. There was a lot of bullying and teasing, and in general he did not see a bright future. Nic constantly wondered why he was different than all the other kids. He was envious and worried how he would have a relationship and marry. He questioned his role in life and if he had a purpose.

But since the age of nineteen he has been a successful motivational speaker around the world. What developed, in spite of the ride he was on, was a new perspective that announces, "No arms? No Legs? No worries!" Then he adds, "No limits." Even though he knew he would never hold the hand of his wife, he focused on holding her heart. Many men with arms struggle to achieve that feat.

Nic makes a daily decision to use his challenges to motivate people. He knows he is strategically positioned to help others who are stuck. Nic quickly removes the barrier for people who do not know how to approach him when he says, "Give me a hug." Suddenly the ice is broken.

Like me, Nic also loves a friendly prank. Recently he donned the uniform of an American Airlines pilot and stationed himself at the door of the jet bridge at the Dallas-Fort Worth airport. He mentioned he would be using new technology to fly the plane as he welcomed passengers aboard. Nic acknowledges his faith in God to help him reach beyond the limits. And like the car keys I keep in my purse, he keeps a pair of shoes in his closet.

Occasionally, I encounter those who really are stuck and in need of rescue. What I find is people often times do not want to be rescued. They like stuck. They hold themselves prisoner. They justify their complaints and their negative attitude. They spend a great deal of energy on the wrong thing. It works for them. But there is only one place it works for them—in their own mind. They must embrace a different perspective, and they must first learn to hate stuck.

Each day is a gift and tomorrow a hope. Staying stuck in the fears of yesterday locks you out of the joy of this moment. Position yourself to enjoy today. Stuck in the wrong mindset makes you your own prisoner. Hate the stuck that limits your life. Live free.

Position yourself to enjoy today. Each day is a gift and tomorrow a hope. You're not stuck—you've been positioned.

CROSSROAD

Years ago when I was single, my family and I traveled to the Middle East with a group of friends. One day, an Egyptian merchant approached my Dad and offered him seven camels in exchange for me. Recently, I called my dad and asked, "Dad, why didn't you take his offer?" Dad quickly responded, "I'm still kicking myself for turning him down!" As humorous as it seemed on the surface, I couldn't help but wonder if seven camels were a fair market price, or perhaps a deep discount. I remembered another time that my parents had refused an offer for me when I was just a baby. A six-year-old boy offered them six silver dollars, his entire life savings. The little tyke just wanted his own baby sister. I'm happy to report that I am much more expensive now. Just ask my husband. In a disposable world where life has been sorely devalued, what does a life cost anyway?

My husband's name means priceless one. He certainly is of great value to our family, and his faithfulness is like gold. The dictionary definition of the word "tony," is luxurious or expensive. Hence, only the toniest resorts are featured in travel magazines. Everyone's name should remind them of their own pricelessness, yet far too many feel worthless and stuck. I am all too familiar with the train of damaging thoughts that can undermine a person's sense of worth.

I never wanted to be stuck as a blind woman. Words cannot accurately describe the devastating loss I experienced when my eyesight gradually diminished. The mental battle was more devastating than my declining vision. My number one fear was the loss of my perceived value. How could I ever be the wife my husband needed and deserved? How could I ever be the mother my children needed and longed to have? And, who was ever going to call on me to carpool?

I also feared the barrier between others and myself due to what the world would call a disability. Most able-bodied folks do not know how to engage people with disabilities and often take great strides to avoid them. On the other hand, some who try to engage say or do silly things. I wonder if they even realize it. People with no impairment often think they do me a kindness by saying, "I know exactly what you are going through." I seriously doubt it.

Here's my short list of some humorous attempts to assist me with my impairment: A hotel clerk offered to give me a handicap room for the visually impaired equipped with a special strobe light. I have been offered special seating with the deaf because there would be someone there to do sign language. I can only be grateful for the many books given to me as gifts, but, no, I haven't read a single one. There are those who wave at me and think I'm stuck up because I don't wave back. Then there's the other friend who offered to take me to the grocery store and attempted to let me out at the curb with the promise to pick me up later. I have been asked if I hang out with blind people, and I simply reply, "No, someone has to drive."

Sometimes people think if they talk louder I will understand them better. It's not my hearing but my eyesight that is impaired. Still others think they do me a favor by pointing to the menu, nodding their head to affirm something I said, or extending their hand to offer a handshake. When I speak to an audience I don't ask for a show of hands. Sorry, I don't see any of it. If you have plans to be my friend—you'll just have to talk to me.

My dreams and life plans have changed drastically because of my diminished eyesight; yet, at the end of the day more has been attained than lost. I couple my story with humorous lines and real life tales, because it breaks up the depth of sorrow that would keep me crying the rest of my life. The exchange for me has been a focus on what I still have. I have discovered that sharing my life view and my life message challenges others to take a closer look at their lives.

Still, the feeling of living a devalued life is a constant struggle, but I am learning how to walk free with joy. It first started as a game to keep me from the pits of depression. Every time I felt I was stuck in blindness I thought about a blind world groping for answers, impaired by shortsightedness, disabled because they *think* they can see. I began to realize that most visual people see what they want to see and deliberately overlook what they refuse to believe.

The day I realized that I had been living in a blind world was the day my sense of purpose and self-worth were restored. I often say and believe, "Visual people are high maintenance." They won't go anywhere unless they can see the end results. They won't believe unless they see. In many, the *real* disability is in having eyes that function correctly but fail to envision what cannot be seen with the naked eye.

In times past, when I felt myself spiraling downwards due to sadness, I would call someone to cheer them, or write an email or text to see how I could encourage them. Now it's a lifestyle. I look to see what others are missing and connect it to real life inspiration and teaching moments. In my world, all of it connects. It has made me who I am today.

However, I do not want to stay here. I want to keep growing and reaching. In my world everyone has value. No matter how irritating their personality, or how annoying the individual appears, wealthy or impoverished, from the oldest to the youngest, they each have value. Life is priceless and so is each person—including you.

My limited eyesight creates an advantage. I'm not distracted by what I see. This allows me to focus on matters of the heart and ask the deeper questions.

I stood at the airport waiting to board the plane. Earlier, I had started a casual conversation with the man in line behind me. I asked, "What do you do with your life?"

He cheerfully replied, "Do you mean what do I do?"

"No. What do you do with your life?"

He said, "I have never had to think that deeply before. I've never been asked a question like that."

I softly said, "I can wait."

The world has exchanged what we *do* for who we *are*. One is dispensable while the other is irreplaceable. I am curious. What do you do with your life?

My imagination is fierce and I, too, see what I want to see. I'm everyone's best friend. To me, everyone looks great: thinner, younger, and destined to live a big life. The real shock will be when I see again, because I love what I see when it comes to you. I'm sure I won't be disappointed.

Here are some other advantages to my blindness. To me, my husband still looks like the same young handsome man I married years ago. I've totally missed the aging changes of my elderly parents and all their gray hair. I'm bothered less by distractions, and I decided long ago that not seeing everything my children have done is probably a blessing. I am also colorblind, and I hope I never recover from this affliction. I am not moved by what you wear, or what you drive, or where you live. I am not moved by how much money you have, or by the precious jewels that adorn you, or the name brand clothing you sport. I am only moved by your attitude and how you smell. And, sometimes both of those stink. But both can be refreshed.

I frequently come back to the topic of value, and I wonder if this is where you struggle as well. The details of your story are different from mine, but perhaps life has tarnished the shine of your smile and dimmed the hope of a better day. To live stuck in the belief that you do not count or that your worth is not enough to matter is true blindness. Won't you please let me help you find your way on the dark path you now walk?

I am fully confident that your value is not connected to economics and how much you can add to the Gross National Product. Your value is not merely how many friends you accumulate or how many times you volunteer for important causes. Your value is not politically determined by how effectively you can paint your philosophies on the minds of others. Your value is not religious and how many traditions you embrace. Your worth remains constant. There are no plus or minus columns, just value and priceless worth.

If your value is based on your position, what happens when there are cut backs and layoffs? A paycheck is always underpayment compared to your own personal worth and the hours you invest. Determine now the real value of who you are and what you bring to your world, to your position, and to your family. Make your very life your gift. Focus on your output instead of your income.

If your value is contingent upon the applause of others, the things you own, or the house in which you live, you will always feel insecure. Please keep these things in mind: A change can be forced upon you through a storm, a fire, or a bankruptcy. Positions and fame come and go with the turn of markets, mergers, and consolidations. Aging has an interesting way of trying to erode your sense of worth. Despite the harsh realities of aging, it alone has no power to change your core value.

If your value is determined by your spouse, your family, or who you think you should be at any particular age, think again. Some feel less than priceless because they are single and have no one to partner with them in life, while the married person could look back with envy at the freedom of the single life. The barren grieve over their empty arms, feeling cheated of children, while another family resents having no privacy because they feel suffocated by all their children and all the crazy schedules. The older try to look younger, while the pre-teen tries to look older. The pressing question remains: are you satisfied with your worth?

Comparisons will always threaten to diminish your self-worth. You can always find someone in a better or worse situation than the one you are presently in. Your infinite value cannot be determined by comparing yourself to others. Your life is valuable all by itself. Don't compare it to someone else. Just move forward.

What has devalued your opinion of yourself? If it's your past failures, look to new opportunities. If you were born on the "wrong side of the tracks," then move—just don't take a miserable mentality with you. If you're continually unhappy, seek to find joy in something less fickle than the circumstances of life. If you lack training, then get the education and skills you need. If you are blind, then hear what most overlook. If you are deaf, sharpen your eyes to see beyond what most hear. If you are lame, then team with runners in life who are champions. If you are bruised, help those who are broken in your midst. If you are bored, then help someone who is overwhelmed. If you are sad, then write down your blessings and rejoice.

A mind is changed one thought at a time. An outlook is changed one viewpoint at a time. A life is changed one decision at a time. A course direction is changed one degree at a time. Decide what you are willing to leave behind in exchange for living your dream. Then, get up and live!

My friend Cindy was at the airport preparing for her flight. She felt good about herself and loved what she was wearing. In fact, she had convinced herself that she looked really cute for a day of travel. But my friend's view of herself was limited by what she could see in the mirror. Cindy stood at the ticket counter selecting her seat assignment, when a gentleman tapped her on the shoulder.

"Excuse me ma'am. I was about to put this picture on YouTube, but decided to tell you instead."

Cindy leaned in to look closely at the display on his cell phone, only to be told, "Ma'am, you have the paper toilet seat cover stuck in the back of your pants."

A 360 degree view of your life often requires the aid of another set of reliable eyes. What others see is not what we see. Take the time to step back and see the good that has already come to your life. Soak in the big picture and fill in the gaps. Marvel at how far you have already come from where your journey began, lest you feel overwhelmed by the distance you still need to travel.

While writing this book, I sat at my computer in the middle of the night with the lights out and my monitor off. I asked myself, "What is the ultimate depiction of my premise—Stuck or Positioned?" The answer that came unnerved me. I considered an innocent man, a splintered cross, and an unjust execution. Jesus Christ was hung between two thieves and stuck with mankind's sin. Was this a cruel joke?

No matter your background or belief system, you must not overlook what happened at this crossroad in history. The passion of Christ contains the most remarkable message ever communicated between God and man and is studied even by those who do not embrace its worldview.

The story is genius.

God sent His only son, Jesus Christ, to die for the sins of the world. His innocent Son gave up His life for ours.

Nails were driven through His hands and feet. He was thrashed, beaten, and ridiculed, and a makeshift crown of thorns cruelly punctured His brow. Yet, astonishingly, He cried out, "Father, forgive them for they know not what they do." Surely His suffering and final words caught the attention of his accusers. But above all, His plea reverberates across time and knocks on the door of every person—even now.

Make no mistake—they did not take His life. He gave it. And with resolve, He proclaimed, "It is finished."

From His finish we now begin anew, never to be without His presence. Man's failings collided with God's unmerited favor. God, in His mercy, paid an extravagant price for you and me. Here, reconciliation to a holy God is found. Three days after His death, Jesus rose from the grave. Hope now lives eternal with the supernatural power to resurrect and renew our dreams for tomorrow, and provide the fresh empowerment we enjoy daily.

His sacrifice was an incomprehensible act of unconditional love for mankind. Was Jesus *stuck* on a cross for humanity, or was He strategically *positioned* to save? The answer is, "Yes." He was uniquely positioned to die in our place. And, having risen from a borrowed grave, He is positioned evermore at the right hand of God the Father.

The outcome of His extravagant gift is that you and I can know personal value beyond our wildest dream, beyond all earthly currency and comprehension. However, the gift has little value if not received and opened. I am curious, "Are you stuck in unbelief, or are you positioned to say, 'Yes,' to the One who is Life Himself?" New life is yours—if you want it.

You may be familiar with this marvelous story, but did it ever occur to you that it cannot have a happy ending without your personal involvement? Your value is established by the Life given on your behalf. You're not stuck—you've been positioned.

RELEVANT

In 1998 during the Atlantic tropical storm season, category 5 Hurricane Mitch developed into the deadliest weather event since the Great Hurricane of 1780. Honduras was its principle target, and it is a wonder that anyone survived. Staggering measurements reported sustained winds of 180 miles per hour with wind gusts measuring 200 miles per hour. Seventy-five inches of rain fell in four days, causing floods and mudslides that washed away entire villages, while the majority of the country's crops and infrastructure were decimated. The region confirmed 11,000 dead and an equal amount missing. Nearly twenty percent of the nation became homeless. The hurricane destroyed 150 Honduran bridges, but in the middle of the destruction one bridge remained, The Choluteca Bridge. Miraculously, this marvel with its white concrete sculpture and graceful arches survived.

No wonder the Japanese still brag of the bridge that withstood this horrific storm. They built it in the 1930's as a gift to the Hondurans. Its structure was sound, but it is irrelevant now. It may have endured the storm, but it now leads nowhere since the hurricane redirected the river it used to span. The architects and builders of this great bridge brought a design forward that served the people of that region well for several decades. One major hurricane turned this bridge into a simple statue.

This causes me to wonder how often we praise our self-made organizations and businesses without noticing if they are still effectively serving the needs of others. The architectural plans of any idea must have people at the center of its purpose, if it is to remain relevant. People are our business.

Businesses are about people. Ministry is about people. Families and marriages are about people. Education is about people. Too often we are distracted by the sheer genius of our plans, and completely lose sight of why an idea, a concept, a strategy, a business, or a bridge even exist.

Once I was asked what I wanted more than anything in the world. Assuming I would answer, "To see again," I surprised them. As much as I would love to see again, my honest answer remains, "I want to be effective." Could there be any greater success than effectiveness? True effectiveness makes a relevant impact on the world in which we live.

Believe it or not, one of the most energetic audiences I have encountered was composed of a large group of cowboys and cowgirls. In fact, the "Cowboy Church" movement in our country is one of our country's fastest growing social phenomena.

I was recently invited to speak for a large cowboy church in east Texas. In preparing for that event, I asked Jason, one of the founding members, how this church of over one thousand got its start. He said it all began one Sunday when he and his family were sitting in the balcony of their traditional church. Jason had ranched all his life and he had the big hat and boots to prove it. His dusty career was filled with early morning cattle chores, pinning and roping cows, as well as all of the responsibilities associated with countless acres. His breed is one-of-a-kind, and they are rarely found in an uptown church.

One day a man stood in the choir with a burning desire for relevant outreach. He happened to look up at the balcony while singing.

94

That's when he saw his buddy, Jason. At the end of the service, the man approached Jason and asked him, "Where are your people?"

Jason asked, "What do you mean?"

The man asked again, "Where is your kind?"

Jason replied, "Not in church this mornin'. They're either workin' or recoverin' from last night."

In short order, this community leader asked Jason to help him start a cowboy church in the area. This expanding work reaches people in blue jeans who work hard and have the reputation of living "raw and real." Jason eventually became the cowboy church pastor and calls his work a trauma center to help those who have been assaulted by life and have lost their way.

The outreach to these ranch communities is housed in a barn-like building surrounded by a big arena for outside events. From rodeos to bull rides to other cowboy extravaganzas, these pioneers have struck a nerve where people live. No longer content to preach to the choir, these ministers get their hands dirty working side by side. Transformed lives are the indisputable evidence of their work's relevance.

Another type of community outreach I appreciate is found in the loving efforts of those who work in Women's Resource Centers across our land. These dedicated folks work on the front lines of life, helping women and families make informed choices about unplanned pregnancies. Here, communities pool their funds to supply a safe place to receive counsel, loving concern, and practical help. A wide range of medical tests is provided, including pregnancy tests. Most of these centers offer education for birthing, parenting, and early childhood development. Complimentary sonograms allow a woman to see the child growing within her womb with the hopes that innocent life will not be terminated. More support is given in the form of food and clothing, diapers, and practical resources.

These vital support teams are funded by donations and staffed by dedicated volunteers. Some centers also network with adoption agencies and legal centers. Post-abortive counseling is also offered at many life centers to help a woman move from regret to wholeness. In other centers, housing is made available, coupled with further education and life skill training.

One such center on a major university campus in the East expands their outreach by offering young ladies rides back to their housing or dormitories in the early morning hours. The girls are awaking from their "walk of shame." Too often, they have nothing on their back but a borrowed blanket and are not even sure how to get back to their dorm. This unexpected kindness is welcomed by most. The mornings after are met with a caring ear, if a girl wants to talk. A lost night of blurred passion often turns into a rude awakening. This is a far cry from the condemning voices of yesteryear, which judged too freely and offered no real help. I applaud relevant and noble efforts to keep the needs of women and their babies a central focus.

We live in a day when anything that can be challenged will be challenged. For instance, some argue that the Bible is irrelevant. How can a book that has been on the top seller's list for centuries be irrelevant?

If you read the Bible you will find information on: philosophy and psychology; religion; social sciences; languages; science; technology; arts and recreation; literature; as well as history and geography. The Bible comments on all of life's major topics: agriculture; astrology; botany; biology; business; communications; criminology; death and disease; divorce; economics; human resources; government; history; humility; illness; justice; law-making; leadership; life; marriage; morality; nation building; personal development; personal responsibility; redemption; pageantry; sociology; superstition; sexuality; warfare. It speaks to individuals, marriages, families and communities. Nations have been impacted by the Bible's influence.

The reason some announce that the Bible is irrelevant is because they don't want to answer to its Author or answer to the next generation for not telling them about its wisdom. Comfort, challenge, and conviction are found throughout its pages. Leadership, relationships, and eternity are mingled within the chapters. Purpose and design, along with life-giving words, are throughout the Bible. Truth is timeless. And absolute truths are always relevant, no matter the calendar year or shifting philosophies.

Philosophical relevance is challenged every day in China by people of faith. By some estimates, there are over 100 million Christians in China today. The Communist party in China requires its members to be atheist, and they keep a political thumb on people who don't adhere to their teachings. Nevertheless, those under the thumb have grown significantly. What goes on in China is a testimony that the most relevant things of life grow best under pressure. Chinese Christians, quietly and measurably, move their way into the culture, like a small amount of yeast makes its way into an entire lump of dough.

In 2011, Norway had an interesting phenomenon visit its culture. This Scandinavian country is called "secular" Norway for obvious reasons. The Bible Society of Norway took current events from the news, including foreign affairs, family, taxes, and education, and distributed Bible verses across the nation, addressing each of these subjects and more. However, they did not reference the Bible in the process. The general public started to respond, saying this was great stuff—really smart—and asked where the advice came from. Eventually, the Society admitted it came from the Bible. As a result, the Bible became the bestseller in Norway that year.

The Bible is so relevant that, as a culture, Americans enjoy using 257 Bible-based idioms on a daily basis. Here is a small sampling: a fly in the ointment; by the skin of your teeth; I'll give you my two cents worth; a leopard can't change its spots; the writing on the wall;

there's nothing new under the sun; thorn in the flesh; the sign of the times; from the cradle to the grave.

A famous brain surgeon revealed the key to his success in a recent interview. He said, "I read a chapter of Proverbs every morning and at the end of the day." He expressed that the wise counsel and wisdom he found there informed his life and were relevant to each day of his career. By reading a chapter of Proverbs each day of the month, the thirty-one chapters are perfectly structured for daily motivation and inspiration. Try reading Proverbs for a few months and see if your eyes are opened wider to expanding wisdoms.

Raymond is a close friend who owns a sandpaper distribution company. On an industrial level, the products manufactured there are called abrasives. Raymond told me that almost everything I have ever touched needs abrasives to complete the production. As common as sandpaper is, it still maintains its relevance on my cabinets, desks, and counters. It shines anything made of stainless steel, from my toaster to automobiles and hair dryers. Light fixtures, fireplace mantels, doors and handles, all have had some varying grades of sand paper run over them to give them a smoother, polished feel and look. Though we joke that it might be a "rough business that rubs people the wrong way," the truth is, the abrasive industry touches the world. Realizing the significance of sandpaper, he expanded his business. Our "abrasive" friend decided to buy out one of his manufacturers and moved from buying and reselling the products to making them.

One day Raymond and my husband were traveling together down the highway. Raymond told Tony, "Look at everything you can see from our position here on the highway. How much money did it take to produce, manufacture, and construct all you can see?" The exercise powerfully challenged small-minded thinking. Roads, buildings, signs, glass, cars, and everything else represent ideas taken to market over time. Each of the entrepreneurs behind these visible products at some point had to overcome risks, shortage of funds, people telling them it would not work, and other changes in the marketplace. Pressing through all those obstacles, they became relevant in order to serve others in ways both rewarding and profitable.

New discoveries and inventions redefine relevance. Old typewriters and carbon copies got the job done, but computers and other digitally-based equipment have left them in the dustbin. Henry Ford had good ideas for his day, but because many other new and improved ideas have come along since, the Model T finds its limited relevance in museums.

Over lunch one day, another friend, David, pointed out that the games of chess and checkers are played on the same board. Many love checkers. It is fast moving and easy to make the jumps toward the big win. It reminds me of all the hoop-jumping that life can demand. Are the real victories of life a pattern determined by the expectations of the crowd, or are there strategies, like a chess game, that can take us to new levels of influence? Living or doing business like everyone else is status quo, but what if you were to strategically think of ways to effectively serve others?

The most successful businesses, universities, restaurants, and hospitals have taken on a strategy-based way to reach into the marketplace. If you intentionally seek a pertinent strategy, soon it becomes a lifestyle. Your focus is to embrace the journey, and every day your goal is to be effective in all you do. Staying relevant means staying in touch with strategies that challenge and transform your life, your business, and your reach.

How important is personal relevance? If you don't vote, how relevant are you in the political process? If you don't communicate, how relevant are you in your relationships? Are you a bridge that is of great practical use, or are you only the statue of a bridge and your contribution is no longer pertinent? When your own relevance is shallow or undefined your entire life will tend to be superficial. Instead of enjoying life, you babysit it. Are you a giver or a taker?

What if you became a resource for others? Your relevance is measured by how much you contribute, not by how much you accumulate. Your deepest sense of relevance is also measured by how well you draw people out of themselves so they can thrive.

Reevaluate your effectiveness. Be intuitive in changing times. Decide to be relevant. You're not stuck—you've been positioned.

WELLS

Do you feel you are living in the shallow end of life, lingering where it is comfortable, but never really feeling refreshed? The problem with the shallow water is that you are only partially committed to the pool, and you can't dive in without going brain dead.

But if you are brave and head to the deep water where you cannot touch the bottom or reach for the sides, you will develop your skills and discover a new sense of challenge and intrigue. Deep water offers plenty of room for self-discovery, innovation, and creativity. Your talents will never be fully realized while splashing in a few inches of water.

I love the proverb, "Deep calls to deep." In case you think this is only for a certain few, do not be fooled. Everyone can go there—if they want. It is in the deep places where we learn to trust. You may tread water for a while, but eventually you will find the motivation to do something different. Anyone can linger in the small places of shallow thinking and living, but the courageous search for more. The answer you seek may be closer than you imagined.

There is an anecdote that Booker T. Washington used in his Atlanta Compromise speech in 1895. It was about a crew of men who were lost in a ship off the coast of South America and had gone days without drinking water. Thirst threatened their lives. As a ship passed by they signaled for help. Their cry was for fresh water. The sailors on the passing ship told them, "Cast down your buckets where you are." But the thirsty crew knew they couldn't drink the seawater.

The thirst-ravished men signaled again for fresh drinking water. Once more the men on the passing ship signaled for them to drop their buckets where they were. Bewildered and desperate, they finally drew buckets from the sea that surrounded their ship. The water was saltless and refreshing. They later discovered they were on top of fresh water the whole time. The men were at the mouth of the Amazon River that fed into the salty sea.

Many overlook the treasure on which they are sitting. What could be under your nose in the position you hold that could answer your need? Instead of dying of thirst for something new in your life, or experiencing a change from where you presently feel stuck, drop your buckets where you sit and discover the potential solutions around you.

Similar stories abound. My grandmother would never have found a large sum of cash my grandfather had stashed in his workshop had she not been searching for a specific tool years after his death. The bitter tragedy of not knowing what you could have had, while doing without, is indeed disconcerting.

What about your own life? What do you have in your repertoire of skills and talents that could potentially deliver you from a life of lack and despair if you would just tap into them? Can you imagine your life changed forever?

"Your gift will make a way for you," is the promise of a wise proverb. What is your gift and when did you last draw from it? Have you explored the very gift that resides in you? Have you overlooked some resource? Is there someone within your network from whom you could glean insight and wisdom? Expand your reach into the world around you.

I once spoke at an oil investment firm. After my presentation, people were milling around visiting with one another before they returned to their offices. I asked the man next to me, "What's the greatest challenge your company currently faces?"

"Dry wells," he responded. He went on to tell me his name was Sean and that he was the Director over Investor Acquisitions and Portfolio Development. He was also responsible for finding the investors and notifying them if the well was dry or good. He had recently made hundreds of calls on a drilled well that was unfortunately determined to be a dry well, Needless to say "dry wells," were fresh on his mind. I didn't know much about drilling for oil, but I knew dry wells are not the desired goal. I reached out and said, "Give me your hand." Never bowing my head, I just asked, "God, give this company a strategy they have not yet seen." Sean quickly excused himself to go back to his office, and I never gave it another thought.

Six months later I was asked to come back to speak to their team of officers, managers, and sales force. Before I was introduced, Tim, the owner and top executive, said, "Gail, we have something to tell you." Tim set the stage by retelling the events of the previous meeting. Then he turned it over to Sean who told the rest of the story. Sean read word for word what I had said and prayed that day. He even documented the date and time. I smiled with great interest to hear what happened next.

The two ping-ponged back and forth, telling me that dry wells had indeed been a growing concern for them and their investors. Not long after I spoke there they called a strategy meeting and a new idea came forward. Some adjustments were made in the drilling process. Their original goal was to get a three pay zone production. However, they received ten pay zones from three wells. This was oil investment jargon to communicate that the increase was out of this world.

Could it be some of our failures are just aborted missions we abandoned too early? In the midst of life's perplexities, have you considered looking at all the angles and possibilities—and even pray? In losing my eyesight I would be a fool to believe that what I cannot see does not exist. My view *is* limited—but so is yours. Sometimes you must fall back and gather your strength and resolve before trying again from another position or place. Often, the level where we need to go will take more effort than first calculated; just give it all you have and then trust that it is enough. If not, recover and try again. Refuse to quit. Listen and quiet yourself as you think, wait, and pray. John Quincy Adams once said, "Duty is ours; results are God's."

A proverb says, "Wisdom rests deep in the heart of him who has understanding." Talk about a well of truth and insight. What are some of the wisdoms that rest deep in your heart's well? Some of mine are: good is the enemy of best; life is more than survival; choices have consequences; storms are not fatal; light dispels darkness; hope is more than a wishful thought; wisdom is the ability to discern difference. I make a conscious effort to draw from my well daily and use the truths and wisdoms revealed over time to empower my life.

Long ago there was a father who dug some wells and then, for whatever reason, abandoned them. Many years later, his son returned to those wells only to find them filled with dirt and debris. He had a choice to make. Walk away, or put forth a concerted effort to clean them out. He cleared them of the trash, and the water flowed freely again. The wells attracted a community, and many were refreshed. He did this over and over until it was said of the man's son, "He prospered, and *is* prospering, and will continue to be prosperous." Safeguarding the value of his father's wells proved to be a satisfying exchange for his hard work.

The same is true in your life. Remove the debris that pollutes your well. You are not meant to be unproductive or short on capacity. Dig a little deeper and put forth more effort. You are presently surrounded by more than you can see. Your attitude may be cluttered with junk. Clear your mind of doubt and negativity. What is the payoff to live with a cynical or critical attitude? Is this negativity a smokescreen you hope will cover up what you don't want others to examine? If you're not careful, you could conclude that you don't need that much water and deny yourself of a deep, productive well. When you look only on the surface you can easily underestimate the mighty underground river that feeds your well. Drill down—go deeper.

I am often asked, "Gail. How can you not see but have so much joy?" I wonder, "How can you see and have no joy." My joy springs from a strong underground current. It's a force that is not dependent on happiness or circumstances. I love the promise that when you "draw from the well of salvation you will have joy." My joy is based on a personal faith and a strong sense of purpose. Your passion will fuel you, and your purpose will drive you.

There's an old story of a farmer who was disgusted with his stubborn mule. In his anger, he threw his mule into a dry well and left him to die. But the mule turned a deficit into an asset. He lived in spite of his owner.

How did he survive? The mule hit the jackpot because many people used the dry well as a dump. Each day, people came to throw their trash, scraps, and junk into the well. They never heard his cries for help, but their actions provided what the mule needed most— some leftover food and something to stand higher on. The mule persistently shook off all the trash and debris thrown at him as he continued to climb to higher ground.

The well-nourished mule used his elevated position to, in time, walk out of his hole into a new level of freedom. If he can do it, you can too.

Life may bombard you with its debris, but you can step up and find a new way to live—on purpose, with purpose, and for a purpose.

Did you know a well is different from a cistern? One has limits while the other is limitless. One draws from an unseen underground source, while the other is merely a holding tank. One is ever-replenished, while the other grows stagnant. I believe you have an inner well of limitless potential from which to draw. You have something to contribute that others can enjoy. You're not merely a holding tank where you have to limit yourself lest you run short.

The words we use expose the depth of the wellspring that is in our heart. To know what's in a person's heart, simply listen to the words that come out their mouth. Is profanity merely proof of a small vocabulary, or an indication that your speech lacks merit without it? Then there is speech that reveals complaints, bitterness, and bad attitudes. A wise elderly friend once told me, "When others speak, listen beyond their words to the cries of their heart." The wellspring of the heart is telling indeed.

My father often traveled to Europe for business. On one particular trip he flew from Chicago to Hamburg, Germany. While cruising at 40,000 feet above the ocean, the airline engines suddenly went silent. The plane plummeted, causing items to fly in every direction. Dad reached out to help a woman and two children near him get safely buckled in their seatbelts. After a few terrifying seconds, the engines reignited. When I asked him how the passengers reacted to the sudden free fall, he said there were three distinct reactions among those onboard. One group screamed, another group yelled profanities, and a third group prayed, calling aloud for God's help.

Author and speaker, Norman Williams, had a similarly chilling experience in-flight on March 27, 1977. Seventy miles off the coast of Northwest Africa among the Spanish Canary Islands, five hundred eighty-three people lost their lives when two 747 jumbo jets collided on Tenerife Island's foggy runway. There, the small town of

Santa Cruz provides a regional airport called Los Rodeos which is surrounded by volcanoes and cascading hillsides. Norman Williams miraculously survived the explosive inferno. However, I have friend whose mother did not.

In his riveting account, Mr. Williams speaks of what shocked him the most about that gruesome scene. Many cursed God, and the recordings on the black boxes were filled with profanities from the cockpit of both planes. Mr. Williams had always assumed a person facing death would naturally call out to God for help. His gripping testimony of survival causes us to consider human behavior under pressure. He concludes that unless conscious changes are made, people tend to die the way they live.

The well of your personal life may need some debris removed. You may need to seek out the proper environment, or other people that can effectively help you remove the stagnation and contamination. I am sure that fresh, living water from deep underground springs can be your experience. Just listen to yourself and you decide. Remind yourself that you are responsible for everything that flows in and everything that is drawn out from the well that is you. Once you have safeguarded your inner well, you will be a source of fresh water to those closest to you.

Test the waters that flow from your life. Remove the toxins and debris that dam the spring of life-giving refreshment you are intended to enjoy and deliver. You're not stuck—you've been positioned.

HAY

I often ask people, "Who do you know that I need to know?" It is said that everybody on this planet is separated by only six other people. If this six degrees of separation theory is true, I want to know as many people as possible. The connections you and I make enrich the life we live, but they also advance our purpose and our life message.

You are rarely stuck if you have a thriving network of people. Who is in your network? They are not just for your benefit, but you can connect them with others. An evolving network positions you for grand opportunities. Work your network and see for yourself.

One afternoon my husband came to me laughing. "Did you see the email offer you just received? It's about some hay."

I asked, "What email? What hay?"

He said, "Your cousin has offered you some hay from Missouri, and if you can sell it at a profit to a third party, then we can keep the proceeds for our nonprofit organization."

Our organization is always on the lookout for ways to increase our revenue. It had been a dry season for our organization, and any extra funds could be put to good use. However, I did not expect my prayers for funds to be answered in such a peculiar way. I am a city girl, through and through, and this took me *way* out of my comfort zone.

My husband continued to see the humor in it, but I started flipping through the mental Rolodex of people I had encountered over the past several years. I remembered speaking in a town known as the Cowboy Capital of the world. It didn't take me long to pick up the phone and call the organization where I had given a keynote address.

"Hi, this is Gail McWilliams from Dallas, Texas. I have a strange request. I'm wondering if there is anyone in your area who might need some hay."

Excitedly she replied, "Yes! We all need hay."

I couldn't believe what I heard. "What do you mean, 'You *all* need hay?' "

She went on to explain, "We're in a drought, and everyone around here is desperate for hay to feed their livestock."

Where had I been? I had not comprehended the ramifications of the drought, especially the effect on ranchers. I asked, "How would I contact someone about hay in your region?"

"The couple who own the Hay and Feed Store were at the event where you spoke. They will remember you."

Suddenly, I was on a hayride beyond my wildest imagination. I immediately called the Hay and Feed Store and reintroduced myself to Nathan. I asked him, "What can you tell me about hay?" He helped me understand that hay includes different grasses, or ingredients, which determine the grade of hay you have. Now, my potential customer became my teacher as he instructed me in the basics—Hay 101. I quickly learned not only the grade of hay I had, but the fair market price my hay would bring. And then the big question, "Nathan, now that you know my hay so well, would you be interested in buying my hay?"

He laughed and said I was a quick learner *and* a savvy business-woman. "Gail, bring in a truck load of hay and let me see if I like it. If I do, I'll buy it."

When I hung up the phone, I shouted across the house. "Hey, Tony! I just sold my first truckload of hay!" My husband couldn't believe it. In my ecstatic state, reality set in quickly with yet another challenge. I sold a whole semi-truckload of hay, but I had a problem—I didn't have a semi-truck. How would I get my hay from Missouri to Texas? It did not deter me in the least.

Once again, I flipped the Rolodex in my mind, this time I tried to recall if I had ever met anyone in the trucking business. It soon became apparent I had not cultivated many relationships in this field. I could only think of a gentleman who once worked as an executive in a trucking company in the Midwest. Though my last conversation with him happened some fifteen years previously, it did not matter as I reached for my phone, eager to reconnect with this long lost acquaintance.

It took a great deal of time for me to locate this man, but I will never forget my first conversation with his executive assistant. I told her my whole story and my desperate need for some trucks. She laughed uncontrollably as she considered a blind city girl in search of a fleet of trucks. I waited patiently for her to catch her breath. Still half shocked, and before patching me through to her boss, she asked me to please keep in touch and let her know how my journey ended. Clearly, she was intrigued with my tenacity. Unfortunately, he wasn't able to help me with my need for trucks. I was back to square one. I would face much more laughter before my search for a trucker ended.

I was intrigued, too. I wondered how far this trail would take me. But I was determined to find a home for some hay. My focus shifted from merely helping my organization to seeing a bigger picture. From the time I first learned of the need for hay through my network and that ranchers in my home state were facing a crisis, I wanted to help.

I became proactive. Every time I was on the phone with someone I ended the conversation by saying that I had a problem. Most would ask, "Are you okay?"

I'd reply, "I need eight flatbed semi-trucks in the next few weeks." After that I would either hear thunderous laughter, or a long silence. No one knew how to take me seriously.

A new hay broker's work is a challenge when you have no trucks. But I decided to have fun. My sight may have diminished, but not my sense of humor. To begin conversations about my new ventures, I would ask, "Hay there?" as if to say, "You have any hay there?" I heightened the silliness by announcing my favorite actress is Rita *Hay*worth, my favorite author is Tim La*Hay*e, and my favorite pastor is Jack *Hay*ford. I had a bad case of "hay-fever" and loved it. I even went so far as to rename my favorite chips—Frito-*Hay*.

Okay, so it got a little crazy.

I continued to struggle to find someone I knew in the trucking industry and realized there are so many people in life I had yet to meet. Meanwhile, I concentrated on the resources placed in my hands. It was only a few days later that I found my answer.

I got a hot tip one night about a trucker who lived in Missouri, just two miles from my cousin's farm. He worked for a large trucking firm based in St. Louis, but his house was right next door to my hay. I quickly called him to see if we could do business. My network was growing one conversation at a time. I explained to my potential driver where my hay needed to be delivered, and we agreed on a price. I will never forget telling him I had lost my eyesight. I thought I heard the oxygen go out of his lungs.

"How do you even know if your hay is good?" He asked.

"Oh, I know it's good because I trust the farm where it's coming from." On his own, he actually went down to meet my cousin, inspect the hay himself, and determine how many bales he could transport.

I continued to work out the details with my new trucker friend, Greg. We picked the date and the time we would meet at a particular truck stop north of Dallas. But first I had one more request of my trucker. "Greg, I will bring your money on one condition." He was silent as I continued. "I want to sit in your rig when I meet you at the truck stop."

He gave a hearty laugh and said, "It's a deal."

My hay was on its way. The bales were about one thousand pounds each. They were round and netted, comprised of orchard grass, red clover, and fescue. They had been conditioned and had never been wet. Along the way people tried to flag down the truck and give cash to Greg to buy my load of hay on the spot. Thankfully, Greg was an honest man who stayed true to our agreement. Greg dropped off the first load of hay to Nathan at the feed store. My "sight unseen" deal was met with approval.

By late afternoon, we rendezvoused at the truck stop in Anna, Texas. He came wheeling into the parking lot and backed his rig in like it was a toy truck. He got out of the rig and met me in the parking lot. I handed him the envelope of cash. He counted out the money. He shook my hand and pointed up to the tractor cab of his semi and said, "It's all yours."

I was clueless how hard it was to climb up into the cab of a semi-truck, but my husband gave me a boost. Soon I sat in the driver's seat with a big smile on my face. Greg climbed in the passenger side and there our conversation began. He said, "Lift your right hand up towards the ceiling and pull on that string." It took me a few moments to find what I could not see. The loud air horn clearly resounded the completion of our first hay deal.

Greg transported a total of eight semi loads of hay for me that season. It was official: I was a hay broker, buying and selling commodities. Throughout this adventure my greatest joy was meeting a new group of people—ranchers and truckers. Both are hard working groups of people whose work is often overlooked and underappreciated.

Who would have thought my original need and a simple offer would eventually develop into resources to help ranchers in crisis?

Your network will help you reach beyond your own ability and stretch your learning capacities. Never underestimate its value.

My friendship with Greg continued that season in the context of a conversation I had while seated with him in the cab of his truck. I turned to him and said, "Your life has great value Greg." He modestly minimized my compliment at first, but I continued, "Greg, whether you deliver a load or pick one up, you are key to commerce. It all rides on you. Thank you for what you do."

I gave him my CDs to listen to while he traveled the highways. Later that year, he came to hear me speak for an engagement close to his home. I had a keen sense this hayride of ours was about much more than just a business deal. Weeks later I received a call from the trucking firm where Greg was based. I was both honored and shocked when the manager asked me to work for their firm.

"Lady. We have never seen *anyone* move so fast and have so many connections across this country." I wish I had asked what my starting pay would be, but I declined before he could pitch his business package. I am convinced that if I can take on the challenges of life, surely you can too. Turn what you do into a memorable ride.

Everyone faces challenges, but few want to put forth the effort to learn something new. Don't let excuses rule when obstacles are present. You will expand your territorial reach when you are willing to grow.

Two years later I was booked in Kentucky to speak in a small community on the Ohio River. Amazingly, my hay business once again became the perfect backdrop while meeting an unpretentious businessman. At the end of the day, we were invited for dinner at a family's home with a few of their friends. I knew most of the people there except for one quiet gentleman named Martin. I sensed he was a man of great insight with leadership qualities. He had attended the meeting where I spoke. He thanked me for giving him permission to do what he does best. His mission and focus is to impact lives in the corporate arena, teaching others to succeed in business.

As we continued our visit we realized we had something in common; we both were hay brokers. Granted, he has done it for more years than I have, but our *hay* connection soon led to a *heart* connection as we talked on for hours that night. His beautiful rolling hills of alfalfa yielded a grade of hay superior to mine, but our respect for each other's "field" quickly grew into the initial connection of our lasting friendship. Truly, there are no accidents in life.

Is it possible you have overlooked entire groups of people because they are not currently in your field of interest? Look for ways to expand your network beyond your normal horizons. By being sensitive to the needs of others, we can turn our seasons of famine into bountiful harvests. Many times helping others will ultimately help us as well.

You may think you are stuck with nothing, but it is not true. Look around to see what you might have dismissed as too hard, too unknown, or too unrelated, and get ready for the ride of a lifetime. You're not stuck—you've been positioned.

ROOF

Originally, our family lived in the Midwest. During those years my husband was the pastor of a church. The church had purchased a vacated school building on three acres of land and was in the process of renovating it into a multi-purpose facility. A watchful eye had to be kept on parts of the flat roof until it could be fully repaired. When it rained water could build up and leak inside. Certain precautions were in place, including a garden hose placed in the lowest section of the roof to help siphon off the unwanted standing water.

Late one autumn afternoon, the weather was threatening rain, with a chill of gusty wind. Tony decided to check the roof before coming home that night. Wearing his dress clothes, he propped a ladder against the side of the building and climbed up to the roof. Everyone else had left for the day, but he felt certain that this task would only take a few moments. But as my husband checked the roof for any pooled water, the wind blew his ladder to the ground.

After some time, Tony discovered his predicament. He stood alone on the roof of the church helpless, and there were no cell phones at the time. Tony moved toward the highest front peak of the roof and surveyed his options. The property was situated near a road, so he began to wave at the motorists who passed by periodically. Most never noticed him, while others simply waved back. It still amuses me to think that passing travelers must have thought him to be the friendliest pastor in town.

Fortunately, one of the drivers who had originally waved to my husband, circled back to check on Tony. He was curious why a grown man would stand on the highest peak of a roof just to wave at people during a rainstorm. He repositioned the wayward ladder and rescued Tony.

Ladders are useful tools when positioned in the right spot. They allow you to climb to higher advantage. Businesses and corporations offer us ladders that can take us to career advancements and ambitious goals. We are exhilarated by business strategies and fiscal maneuvering. We reach for high places to enhance resumes and expand our life experiences. Top rung achievements and peaks in our careers are admired by onlookers.

Many climb the ladder of success with no regard for those they are passing on their way up. They care only for their own ambitions. This tends to distract you from those valuable people you meet along the way, especially those who deserve a great deal of credit for getting you to where you are now.

Once at the top of your own ambitions, do you find yourself waving, but no one notices? How terrible to arrive, alone, at the peak of success. Are you stuck in an attitude that no career advancement or economic success could possibly remedy?

I've heard it said that our destruction is inevitable when the gap is too large between our core, who we really are, and our image, what we hope others perceive us to be. Climbing successfully to the top rung may look great on the outside, but then what? Is there room to lead others? Does anyone really notice how good you look at each of your promotions? What can make the difference?

If you really are at the top, then it seems that there is nowhere to go from there. That must be disconcerting. What if true success isn't defined by how high you can reach, but by how well you reach in all directions?

There is everything right about the momentum needed to move great ideas forward, yet the higher purpose is to make this world a better place. Stephen Covey warns career ladder-climbers to make sure the ladder they are climbing is against the right wall.

Alison Levine inspires others by her physical achievements. She has climbed the peaks of the highest mountains on each of the seven continents, including Mount Everest, where she was a part of the first all-woman team to reach the top. She has skied to both the North and South Poles. This 5'4" dynamo has never allowed a heart defect and nerve damage to deter her from constantly achieving more. She has also proven to be an inspiring teacher, turning her stories of failed climbing attempts into positive life and leadership messages.

One life lesson she shares about her mountain climbing adventures seemed a particularly maddening journey. The idea of an attempt to climb the tallest mountain in the world is intimidating enough, but to find out how it's done is daunting.

The climb to the summit of Mount Everest is not accomplished by starting one day, climbing straight to the top and arriving so many days later. The human body must adjust to high altitudes at a relatively slow pace. This means the climbers of Everest climb for ten days just to arrive at the historic Base Camp. They spend several days here acclimating to the thinner air. There are four more camps between the Base Camp and Everest's lofty summit.

After spending a few days at Base Camp they climb to Camp One, where they spend the night. The next day they descend back down to the Base Camp where they remain for a few more days. Then, they climb back to Camp One. The next day they climb to Camp Two. The following day, they descend to the Base Camp. They remain at the Base Camp for a few more days. The next climb is back to Camp One, where they spend the night, then to Camp Two again, only to descend back to Base Camp for a few more days. They climb back to Camp One, climb the next day to Camp Two, and climb the day after that to Camp Three. Then, you guessed it, they descend once again all the way down to the Base Camp.

The chief objectives of returning so frequently to the Base Camp are rest and hydration. Both are vital as the climbers allow their bodies to acclimate to the higher elevations. Ascension is the obvious goal of mountain climbers, but the routine descent to Base Camp is mandatory. No wonder Alison and her team climbed for two months. Each calculated step up meant another step back down the mountain incrementally moving toward their ultimate goal of arriving at the peak in time.

The heartbreak of abandoning their climb two hundred feet short of the summit during their 2002 expedition was the result of a storm. One might ask then why not just hurry and finish the two hundred feet while so close to the top. But it's not as easy as it may seem. Because of the thin atmosphere and low oxygen levels, every breath is a challenge. Each step forward required stopping to take five to ten breaths, then taking another step. Unfortunately, the conditions were too difficult, and they had to turn back.

But Alison returned eight years later to make another attempt to climb Everest. Again, very similar weather patterns threatened to push her and her team off the mountain. Alison says that, in spite of the storm and without total visual clarity, she realized the best thing she could do was put one foot in front of the other. Following this simple philosophy helped Alison arrive at the summit of Mt. Everest on May 24, 2010. Surprisingly, she says that arriving at the summit did not mean as much as the lessons she learned along the way.

The harsh environment in which Alison learned those lessons included deep vertical walls, treacherous caverns, expanding and contracting ice, and extreme cold. Yet, the pervasive challenge in meeting her goal was the psychological frustration of continually descending, when you are so eager to climb ever higher. She wisely understood that progress was not limited to any particular direction.

It will take true grit to accomplish your dreams and goals. Many times you will feel self-conscious because it seems so many are watching. There are more people tied to your climb than you realize. You may live in fear of their scorn if you fail, but many of them are silently cheering you on. They want to rejoice with you and will draw motivation from your success.

If you still have breath, you are still the best candidate to accomplish your dreams. Beyond the accomplishment of the climb lies the importance of embracing valuable lessons along your journey. Turn your failures into places where you find a renewed sense of purpose. Keep learning from your mistakes. I suspect that many parts of your life have been filled with "one step forward and two steps back." This does not disqualify you from life's expedition. Now that you've heard Alison's story, you should be encouraged to learn just how normal this tedious process is. Your tenacity and determination will one day pay off. Take some time to rest and catch your breath, then, keep climbing!

Re-evaluate your own level of preparedness. Soldiers do not wear golf shoes. Deep-sea divers do not wear metal shields. Runners do not compete while lifting dumbbells. Put on the right attitude. Invest positivity in your team, reflect courage, take on challenges, and develop endurance. If you are not sincere, know that none of these qualities can be counterfeited for long. Be authentic and attentive to the needs of those around you.

Those who wait for perfect conditions will never begin. On the surface, I probably look like the last person qualified to help others see better. This was no truer than when I first lost my eyesight. Before I could help others I first had to learn that the world is blinded with hopelessness and compromised attitudes. Being born without arms and legs, it was unlikely that Nic Vujicic would one day teach others how to dance with joy through life. But, he does it every day. America's most famous quadriplegic, Joni Eareckson Tada, might seem an ineligible candidate to coach others to run circles around their competitors, but she has done it for years. Zig Ziglar said, "Failure is not a person; it's an event." Failure will teach you the value of success. Obstacles will sharpen your creative abilities. Stopping merely marks the starting point where you can begin again.

No matter where you are in your climb of life, acknowledge the valuable lessons and keep going. Equip yourself with persistence, tenacity and a vision for your desired summit. You're not stuck—you've been positioned.

Play

One December our daughter, Lindey, and her family were scheduled for a photo shoot. At first they considered a traditional family portrait. But once the photographer suggested they get some action shots, their creativity soared. Lindey and Ryan decided to turn their portrait into a statement. They quickly rearranged their furniture to showcase the blank wall in their living room and began painting a mural there. Our son-in-law is an artist, and he easily free-handed a sketch of a city skyline. Everyone took a paintbrush—even our young grandson— and worked together. Contrast our 6'3" son-in-law working swiftly as our three-foot tall grandson added flowers and designs closer to the wall's baseboard. Then, Lindey gave the mural lasting significance by painting three words: *Inspire. Dream. Play.*

Lindey says it is hard to inspire others when you are not inspired yourself. I agree. The dividends of intentional deposits can come from wise counsel, books, and listening to seasoned mentors. The Internet helps keep motivational sound bites and video clips at your fingertips.

A man once told me his library is full of biographies and autobiographies. In a few hours of reading he can learn from a life already lived. He builds on the experiences of the lives he studies, while striving to avoid his subject's failures. The most expensive book he ever purchased was two hundred dollars. When asked, "Why would you spend so much on a book?" He answered, "It's a small price to pay for a man's life."

What inspires you? For me, inspiration often comes from the personal challenges of a close friend; the flight of an eagle when he spreads his wings and soars; the struggle of an underdog who wins big; and stories of individuals who overcome the odds.

When inspired, it's easy to dream!

We often quote Martin Luther King, Jr., who boldly proclaimed, "I have a dream…" We admire the dreams and aspirations of others, but we often fail to dream ourselves. If we do dare to dream, we are frequently tempted to doubt those dreams. Past disappointments, failures, unmet expectations, and the required effort combine to create the excuses we need to abort the journey. But, what is your dream worth?

When we were first married, I remember my husband had a literal dream. In his dream he saw the sketched outline of a shopping mall. In it, he could see the framework of every store. As he stood looking into the detailed sketch, one storefront caught his attention. As Tony reached for that particular store's door handle, the entire store came vibrantly alive and seemed real. Your dreams about life are the same. You envision new ideas, businesses, or concepts. But it is not until you reach for them that there is hope for your dreams to materialize, even if, for the moment, the details of your dream are vague.

A dream by itself is non-threatening, but the very nature of a dream demands fulfillment. As a result, many fear reaching into that realm, because a dream may require something of them in the form of sacrifice. But the greatest loss is to never dream at all; to never reach beyond the status quo. I close many email messages with, "Keep reaching—there's more."

Reach again. Dream again.

Weeks later, Lindey shared the insights she gained from that photo shoot with a group of entrepreneurs. One business leader filmed her presentation to share with others. I loved Lindey's first two words, "Inspire" and "Dream." But "Play" I hadn't considered. It is not hard to imagine taking time for favorite pastimes, vacations, and resting, however. Lindey's word "Play" took on more than just the usual meaning. It became obvious that I had misunderstood. She said that her word for the New Year is "Play." "When I put my feet on the floor each and every morning I plan to push 'Play.'"

When I first heard the word play I assumed it meant something different than she intended. I misunderstood because I am not good at playing. I am the daughter of a project engineer. I am always busy with projects, and I have never learned how to play. Resting and playing always seemed like time that could be put to better use, especially when there is a project to finish. Yet both are needed to stay healthy and to maintain a good mental attitude. But Lindey said it best, "I will push 'Play.'" I love that attitude because it is pro-active, visionary, and empowering.

Many live life with their control buttons on mute or pause. Do they even have a play button? I talked with a man once who stated, "All my life I have waited for something to happen." I sadly asked, "All your life?" His dreams and ambitions had been on pause for decades. What keeps you from pushing the Play button and engaging in living your dream? Is your Pause button stuck? Has the music stopped? It's time to press the Play button again. Go ahead, press the Play button. Move forward.

Often the pause we experience is self-imposed. Without a keen sense of our own identity and life purpose, we often hesitate or hold back. You can arrive at a fair estimate of your skills, talents, dreams, and ambitions by taking self-help tests and personality profiles. But it will be impossible to discover your true identity and the depths of your true potential if you do not know the Designer of your life. The One who made you knows you best and possesses the clear picture of all you can be. Get to know Him, and learn more about your true self.

Many find a cause for pause revealed in a phrase nearly everyone uses. It starts like this: "One day I'm going to…" but the "one day" is yet to be written on any calendar. It is usually a wishful thought or announcement that somewhere along the way you had an idea. Your announcement of the idea somehow excuses your fulfillment of it. Your "one day" keeps you resting on pause.

I am often told, "One day I am going to write a book." I reply, "Great. When exactly?" Usually the conversation digresses to their busy schedule, wrong timing, or inability to do the task. By now, I am sure you are not surprised when I say I have more questions for a would-be author. "Are you writing now?" is a good place to start. "In what aisle of the bookstore will I find your book?" "Who is your target audience?" "What is the purpose of your book?" "Who do you want to reach?"

I encourage them to begin writing. Write an email, a blog, a paragraph, a thank you note, or a letter to the editor. Take notes on sermons and business presentations. Just write *something*! All writing is important to an author because to actually write a book requires a great deal of introspection, self-analysis, and relentless attention to detail. It also includes the editing processes for content and grammar, proofreading and rewrites. If you're a writer, begin your dream. Write something.

Many ask me how I became an author and who writes for me. I quickly let them know I write my own books. Then they want to know how. I tell them about my special software program for the visually impaired, and that I can even write in the dark with my monitor off. Each key makes a sound, and the number pad of my keyboard is set up to edit where I can read one word at a time, several paragraphs or pages, at any speed I choose. Having painted the picture of what I go through to write, now you can understand my pain when my first book had 8,000 words cut out of the manuscript during the editing process. I learn to trust my team of editors and our combined goal is a stronger story for all to see more clearly. My autobiography, *Seeing Beyond*, is comprised of a team effort that paid off in time, but it all started with the first paragraph I typed in the dark. Don't tell me you can't. It's time to say you will.

Others tell me, "I want to start a business one day." Again I reply, "Perfect."

I go on to ask: "What is the name of your business?" "Who will you serve?" "What makes your business unique?" "What is your business model?" "Where will your business be located?" "What five people will you hire first for your new business?" "How much profit do you hope to make your first year?"

Some tell me they want to build a house one day. My husband and I also share that dream. After congratulating them on their dream house I ask: "How many square feet?" "Have you sketched out your house?" "What location have you picked?" "How will you use your house in the future?" "Will you sell it one day or pass it on to your children as a tangible part of your legacy?"

Your "one day" can keep you content to live on pause. Go on and push Play and start the process. The most damaging counterfeit to a dream is any comment starting with, "It is too…" This is where your *Pause* button can get stuck. "It is too difficult." Really? Are you going to sing that song with me in your audience? I know difficult. My eyes don't work but I practice seeing. I look to see beyond the difficulties.

The same is true with the phrase, "It's too expensive." Once more, how much does it cost to dream?

"I am too old." Are you still breathing and competent?

"It is too unbelievable." The Bible says, "Be it unto you according to your faith." If you don't believe it can happen, then you won't be bothered with it. Put your unbelief on pause. Release yourself and go on and believe. Time is of the essence.

How much more of life could you enjoy and who could you impact, if only you were not stuck on pause? Go ahead. Push *play*. Dream again. Live again. You have today. Push *play* now.

Push the Play button; start the music, it's time to dance. You're not stuck—you've been positioned.

FLIGHT

Delays are never fun, especially when you're headed home.

I was booked and had completed an eleven-week, eleven-state, thirty-one event speaking tour. My husband typically travels with me but had to return home a week short of my journey's end. We arranged for two of our grown daughters, Holly and Lydia, to accompany me on the last five days of my tour. They were especially glad to join me, as all remaining events were in sunny California.

Regrettably, cold rain was our constant companion each of those five long days. But, together we made many wonderful memories there. Beyond their companionship, they helped carry my bags and work my book table. It was the last leg of a speaking marathon and I was eager to be home for the approaching holidays.

I woke early the final day of the tour. By midday I finished three radio interviews before we headed to the airport. The day had already been busy before we eventually arrived at the small terminal in Bakersfield. I was met with disappointment to hear our plane would not depart on time, due to mechanical difficulties. I fought back tears as I stood at the counter. We were stuck.

In any delay I usually look for surprises and divine connections, but this time I was visibly annoyed. I readily knew the day was hijacked because we would miss every connecting flight from this point to Dallas. My exhaustion was showing, and I felt like I had just enough energy to get on a plane and get home. This was the wrong time to be stranded.

In survival mode, I made myself review the highlights of the past three months, the many wonderful people I met and all the opportunities I was given. These included my good health, the joy of living my dream, and encouraging people from coast to coast. This was my greatest reward. My gratitude for my children and reflecting on the miracle of their lives soon adjusted my poor attitude.

Besides, who wants to be on a plane with mechanical difficulties?

Finally, we were allowed to board a small commuter plane headed to Phoenix. Since the flight was running late, I feared an overnight layover in Arizona. I decided to take it all in stride and the journey continued. The short flight went without incident, and when we arrived in Phoenix we immediately spoke with the airline agents to learn our options.

"There's only one more flight bound for Dallas tonight. It leaves in four hours." I was anything but pleased as four more hours sounded like a week. Another assistant came to talk about rebooking tickets, but somehow the conversation turned toward hairstyles and fashion and great Dallas shopping.

"Girls, let's have a nice leisurely dinner and recap our trip," I suggested to my travel team. The delay actually reduced the pressure, which helped me relax. The meal was fun and soon I realized the gift of the delay was more time with two grown daughters who are normally busy beyond words. As the hours passed I treasured every moment.

After the dinner, we still had time to wait. I was so exhausted I was out of words. I zoned out, staring at people I could not even see. Seated at our newly assigned gate, one daughter watched a movie on her laptop while the other read a book. I sat completely still, numb to the world and too tired to think.

Suddenly, jolted by the jarring announcement coming over the overhead PA system, I heard, "This is the last call for passengers boarding flight 551 to Dallas."

I asked with a tinge of alarm, "Girls! Is that *our* flight?" We jumped to our feet. My daughters ran to two different gates. Holly darted to the counter of the gate where we were sitting. We assumed they had rebooked us. She asked if the McWilliams' are on this flight, to which the agent said, "No." Lydia was already on her way running to the other gate where the announcement had been made for the final boarding to Dallas, Flight 551. I carefully moved to the middle of the airport corridor, positioned to run in either direction.

My face must have shown the stress of that moment because a woman stopped and said, "Ma'am, are you okay?" About that time I heard Lydia yell, "Run, Mom! They're about to close the door to our flight."

Turning, she shouted to the agent, "Hold the door! We're coming." In a dead run, Holly brushed by me and grabbed my arm as we half-flew down the corridor on a mad dash to the gate. It would have made a great scene in an action film. Just like you see in the movies, we miraculously slipped over the threshold of the jetway just as the agent had reached to close the door.

Huffing audibly, we hastily found our seats while everyone stared at us. In a completely full flight it was easy to spot the only available seats. Holly and I sat side by side, and Lydia's aisle seat was two rows behind us. I dropped into my seat and the kind gentleman next to me had already pulled out my seatbelt. He said loudly, "Wow, you must be really important. We came back for you."

"What on earth happened?" I exclaimed. "I thought we missed this connecting flight *hours* ago."

My newest friend explained that the flight *had* left on time, but the mechanical problems that surfaced halfway to Dallas had forced the captain to return to Phoenix. The passengers had deplaned and milled around the terminal for all that time while the repairs were completed. My girls and I had been spared all the mayhem. Instead, we had enjoyed our leisurely dinner and the unexpected time to catch-up with each other's busy lives.

Once settled, I marveled at what had just happened, while my fellow passenger, Mark, talked non-stop. This suited me just fine because I just put my head back and pretended to listen. I am sure I dozed off a few times, but my seatmate did not seem to notice. He proved to be quite the extrovert as he talked on and on about his work, his home, his world travels with his current job, as well as his travels as a Marine. Mark also told me he had never wanted to marry and never wanted any children. His stories helped pass the time.

But the surprises on Flight 551 were only beginning.

Thirty minutes outside of Dallas in our descent, bright lights flashed outside the windows on the right side of the plane. All of us seated in row eleven were unsettled by what we witnessed. Even *I* could see large bright lights were headed towards us at great speed. The Captain's voice broke onto the loudspeakers: "Ladies and Gentlemen, we're in a lightning storm. The lights you see are not an approaching plane." What a comfort! He read all our minds. It looked threatening.

During the descent the effects of the storm were disturbing. We dropped suddenly and the plane rocked. As the turbulence intensified, we were thrown forward. I reached out both my hands to steady myself, grabbing Holly's and Mark's knees.

Moments later it happened again. The plane dropped and swayed. We were thrown forward for the second time, and I grabbed the same knees, only with a firmer grip. The shaken pilot announced firmly, "Brace yourself and hold tightly to your children." The plane again dropped violently when it encountered the sheer winds. Holly took my hand, and I exclaimed, "Jesus!" I asked Mark, "Can I hold your hand, too?"

There I sat, holding Holly's hand tightly and the hand of my new "close" friend, Mark. I'm sure it was a death grip, unlike any Marine had experienced on a domestic flight. It seemed like the descent took forever. Mark had become quiet, probably trying to get some circulation flowing in his hand again, as I instructed, "Keep talking." And he did.

Does your theology allow you to believe in Guardian Angels? Mine does. I am sure I have a fleet of them to get me to my next assignment. It amuses me to imagine them bruised and scraped by all they are called to do in order to help me through life.

I have been stuck many times, and the outcome was not always as glorious as the happy ending on Flight 551. Yet, I trust the process and believe it will all work for good—in time. I remain positioned in expectant hope. Many times people are haunted by the fear they have missed their "golden opportunity." But that's simply not true. Just as the plane returned and picked me up, the vehicle to your next opportunity is circling back to carry you to your desired destination.

A beautiful Creole woman and her macho husband were driving through a blizzard to reach a regional home improvement center. This might seem ludicrous to many, but Jeanette and Ken are a different breed altogether. They live just outside of Bangor, Maine. From their mountainous country lane they could have traveled in any of several directions to reach a hardware store, but that day Ken and Jeanette decided to head away from Bangor to another town. All the schools were cancelled due to heavy snow, so in their adventuresome minds this was a perfect time to gather materials and finish a household project. Jeanette, in particular, needed the distraction of a project to help keep her from worrying about her son, Micah.

Micah was a full-time member of the Army National Guard, and she knew he would be headed home from Iraq within the week. Living near Bangor gave Jeanette an advantage as the citizens of Bangor are famous for their troop greeters who often gather at the airport to encourage troops as they come and go. Bangor International Airport is a common refueling station for military flights departing from, or arriving in, the United States. Jeanette had not seen her son for six months. She had made a pact with one of those greeters who promised to call her whenever Micah's name popped up on the roster of any inbound flights.

As the couple trudged into the hardware store, Jeanette's cell phone rang. Her heart raced when she recognized the voice of her son. Jeanette's friend who greets the troops had noticed his nametag and recognized his face. She handed over her cell phone and said, "Call your mother." If Jeanette wanted to see him she would have to hurry; they would be there less than an hour. As soon as the plane refueled the troops were headed back to their base on the west coast. Jeanette grabbed Ken by the arm and swung him back through the same door they had just entered, "We've got to go. Micah's at the airport!"

Ken drove their Jeep as fast as he dared in blizzard conditions. Interstate 395 was ice-packed and the visibility dangerously low, but Jeanette was oblivious to these obstacles because of her time-sensitive mission. Micah called his mother again to ask where they were.

"Micah! Tell them to hold the plane. *I'm coming!*"

"Amused, Micah said, "Mom, I can't have them hold the flight just for you to get here." But, Jeanette persisted and kept pleading her case.

Just then, Ken lost control of their vehicle and exclaimed, "Oh no! Hold on! Hold on! We're starting to slide!" And, indeed, they did slide off the Interstate down an embankment. Still on the phone, Jeanette yelled her son's name over and over as she screamed, "Micah! Micah! Micah! We're about to crash!"

Micah, surrounded by fellow soldiers, knew his mother was in danger. He was terrified. Many heard Jeanette's screams, and news traveled quickly about their plight. The Jeep flipped one-and-a-half times before landing in an icy snow bank. Jeanette's door was slammed into the snow, but her husband's door was straight up in the air. With a surge of adrenaline, Ken muscled his way out the top of the vehicle and hoisted Jeanette free of the wreckage. Several cars stopped to check on them.

Ken quickly scaled up the slippery embankment and shouted to the first car, "Hey! Are you going to the airport?"

The first driver shook his head, no. Ken said, "Move on." The next couple, on their way home from the grocery store, had watched the Jeep Wrangler slide off the Interstate. Jeanette, shaking and crying, waited while Ken asked, "My wife's son has landed from Iraq and is only here until they refuel. Can you get her there?" The driver responded, "Don't worry, we'll get her there."

When the car finally arrived at the airport's entrance, Jeanette lunged out. The three had not even thought to exchange names. Jeanette's troop-greeter friend beckoned her with a wave and shouted, "They held the plane for you. Hurry! *Run!*"

A long line of troop greeters hurried her along with cheers and applause, whisking her to the correct gate. News had spread quickly of a soldier's mother on her way to the airport to see her son, but was delayed by a car crash. A local newspaper reporter, already at the airport, captured the heartwarming story of their brief reunion. But all the frenzy was a blur to my dear friend. Jeanette only had one thing on her mind; she simply *must* see Micah.

The last call from his mother said she was not hurt but that she would probably not make it in time. Still, Micah was the last of his unit to get back on the plane, hoping to see her. The captain had indeed delayed the flight, awaiting her arrival. Finally, she arrived. Jeanette ran down the jet bridge to the open doorway of the plane. Micah met her with a hearty laugh and a big hug. Jeanette's own laughter was mixed with tears of joy. Then, the whole planeload of uniformed soldiers broke into spontaneous applause as they witnessed the determined reunion of a son and his mother.

Instinctively, Jeanette's big heart and concern for others quickly refocused her attention. She turned briskly, walking down the aisle of the plane, applauding and pointing to the soldiers in each row, saying, "No. You're the ones; you're the ones; you're the ones to be thanked. You're the ones to be applauded." Jeanette celebrated their selfless service by shouting, "Thank you. Thank you. I love you. I love you."

Jeanette and Micah's story landed on the front page of the Bangor Daily News. Jeanette finally found the names of the couple who transported her to the airport and called to thank them. Jeanette's sheer determination far exceeded the blizzard conditions that threatened this mother's hope. Her singular vision for the mission at hand far outweighed all those obstacles. Even though it looked like my friend's goal was unachievable, the key to Jeanette's victory was this: she never stopped trying.

Have you convinced yourself too much time has passed to accomplish your mission? If opportunities have slipped through your fingers, think again. Try again. You're not stuck—you've been positioned.

DELAY

Most of our lives are overbooked and too full to allow for delays and detours as part of life's journey. Few people take the time to "smell the roses" in the garden of life's walkway, because they were supposed to be somewhere else ten minutes ago. All this makes me wonder how much we overlook while hurrying through our jam-packed lives. What surprise nuggets go without discovery as a result?

On the sidewalk during morning rush hour at the Metro subway station in Washington D.C., an unassuming man in a ball cap stood with his violin in hand and its case lying open beside him. He played stirring pieces of classical music for all to enjoy. Sadly, few noticed. Most people walked fast without glancing his way. A few slowed their pace but never fully stopped to enjoy the spontaneous concert. One little boy tried to stop and listen, but his mother grabbed his arm and pulled him along. Now and then a few generous souls threw some change in the violin case. Never had the subway been given such a classical musical memory.

This social experiment was conducted on January 12, 2007. It was the brainchild of a Washington Post columnist who videotaped it on a hidden camera. Of the 1,097 people who passed by, only seven stopped to listen to the musician, and, surprisingly, only one person recognized the famous violinist. Joseph Bell, the violin virtuoso, earned a meager $32.17 for his forty-five minute performance, donated by twenty-seven passersby. Days earlier, Mr. Bell earned much more at the concert hall, where he played the same repertoire. For his insightful journalism, Gene Weingarten won the 2008 Pulitzer Prize for Feature Writing.

I am often frustrated when interruptions derail my plans and agenda. Sometimes, however, I find the courage to let go of the arm that escorts me and stop to enjoy what is happening nearby, in spite of the delay. The other day I was in a quaint village square, and a song I love, played by a live band, could be heard for blocks. I stopped and let go of my daughter's arm. Imagine my surprise when Holly said, "Hey, Mom. You may want to get out of the middle of the street."

I realize some appointments are non-negotiable, and pressing agendas keep us all hopping from one thing to another. It takes intentional effort to not run blindly to the next event on your pre-planned itinerary. You might want to do what I do. My eyes don't work, but I practice seeing. Could it be that at times your eyes don't work either, and you "overlook" the beautiful opportunities around you? These are delays you might enjoy.

Some delays are avoidable, especially when you overlook the details. Our family knows this all too well. Once while traveling to Colorado late into the night, we missed an important turn. Instead of the beautiful mountains of Estes Park at sunrise, we ended up in flat Kansas. What a disappointment to see cornfields when our expectation was snowcapped mountains! We spent most of the day traveling back across Kansas. We overlooked an important detail, which resulted in weariness and disappointment. It left our carload silently fuming.

We finally arrived in Estes Park only to be delayed again. This time, however, by a fascinating scene that was postcard perfect. A large elk stood on the side of the road. We slowed to yield to the impressive animal. The Elk eased its way into the road, and we came to a full stop. Like a school safety guard it held its position, while a long line of younger elk walked slowly across the road. Traffic backed up, while we all waited.

The Colorado trip displayed two different delays and our two vastly different attitudes. One delay left us angry—the other awestruck.

While traveling out West my husband and I held differing views of how we should navigate. I suggested we take a paper road map, but Tony thought his cell phone with its mapping capabilities would be sufficient. He convinced me that paper was a thing of the past, and he preferred the technology. We flew to Denver, enjoyed Steamboat Springs, and then visited Lander, Wyoming. From Wyoming, we planned to meet my brother and his family for dinner in Billings, Montana.

The Rocky Mountains were filled with gorgeous scenery but, unfortunately, phone reception was nonexistent. Access to the high tech map was impossible, and we had left the paper dinosaur at home. Confusion at a particular mountainous intersection left us guessing which way to go. We guessed wrong. When we should have been enjoying a leisurely dinner in Billings, we were at the eastern edge of Wyoming, completely lost. Beyond missing dinner, hours later we arrived in the middle of a major blizzard that forced us to cancel the rest of our vacation.

It is hard to imagine life without cell phones, but there was a day when public pay phones were the only recourse for travelers. Back in those days, our friend Bob was traveling by air and his commercial flight was in the midst of a scheduled layover. He got off the plane to make an important phone call. He intended to keep the call short and return to his seat in plenty of time for the flight to resume. But his phone call turned into a longer delay than intended. Meanwhile, the plane had been refueled and took off without him. Bob was outraged.

Arrangements were made for a later flight, and no one heard from him for hours. When he finally arrived at his business meeting, flustered and annoyed, he was met with ghost-white faces of shock.

"We thought you were dead." They said with alarm. The plane that left without him had crashed.

Mike Huckabee's amazing story of strategic appointments and bends in the road, which elevated him to top positions, should encourage you on your personal path to fulfilled dreams.

Arkansas was a state dominated by Democrats for much of its history. The state has had forty-seven Democrat governors and only six Republican governors. Then, in 1996, Mike Huckabee became the seventh. In large part, his placement was due to a string of strange circumstances, incredibly timed. The governor's story reminds me that *nothing* is impossible.

Governor Huckabee first ran for public office in hopes of winning a seat in the United States Senate. Though he lost that election, he had a remarkable showing for a first political race. Later, Huckabee was urged to consider the run for Lieutenant Governor in the special election when Arkansas Governor Bill Clinton was elected as our 42nd President. Lieutenant Governor Jim Guy Tucker assumed the governorship, and the winner of the special election would become the new Lieutenant Governor. Huckabee won the election.

But he had anything but a warm welcome to his new post. The newly promoted Governor and his staff decided that Arkansas did not need a Lieutenant Governor. The budget for that leadership slot was spent and cancelled out. The office for the Lt. Governor was evacuated. Even the phone lines and the executive office furnishings were removed. For nearly two months the door to the new Lieutenant Governor's office was nailed shut from the inside to deter the newly elected official.

For fifty-six days Huckabee used a corner of the basement coffee shop in the Arkansas State Capital as his temporary office. There he met with concerned citizens and heard their requests. All the while, the new Lieutenant Governor was denied service by the wait staff. Servers in the coffee shop actually turned their backs when Huckabee approached the counter. Under this rude, cruel, and comical childishness, Huckabee remained undeterred. After three court injunctions, Huckabee finally obtained the keys to his executive office and assumed his rightful role as Lieutenant Governor of Arkansas.

After some unimaginable twists and turns in the inner workings of Arkansas politics, this scorned Lieutenant Governor was given yet another promotion. A few years after former Governor Bill Clinton moved into the White House, his successor, Governor Jim Guy Tucker, lost a strategic court battle and was imprisoned, due to his involvement in the Whitewater Scandal. And, as the Arkansas constitution demands, the Lieutenant Governor of Arkansas moved to the office of Governor.

Within Huckabee's first few years as Governor, it was decided that the long-postponed renovation of the Governor's Mansion could wait no longer. Aware of the costly venture, Governor Huckabee made arrangements for him and his wife, Janet, and their three college-age children to move into a triple-wide trailer on the lawn of the mansion. This willing sacrifice of personal comfort and dignity was unlike any made in modern history. This servant leader exemplified how his years in office would look.

Governor Huckabee tirelessly worked for the people and won their hearts. He was reelected twice, serving as the third longest-standing Governor in the history of the state. His peers and his political enemies alike recognized Governor Huckabee's people skills, accomplishments, and leadership. Huckabee was voted to chair the National Governor's Association in 2005. In August of that same year, Hurricane Katrina devastated the neighboring state of Louisiana. Governor Huckabee welcomed more of Katrina's homeless victims than any other state. He called a network of pastors with summer camps and asked them to stay open and help house and feed the homeless.

How do *you* prepare for delays and the unexpected? Are you living with vision? Have you trained yourself to expect the impossible? If so, you are headed in the right direction.

Scott Turner is a firm believer that you must believe in your own dream. Scott expected an invitation in the mail from the National Football League Scouting Combine. The Scouting Combine is where the road to the National Football League begins. It is the division of the NFL that tests a player's speed, strength, and football instinct through numerous drills. However, his invitation never arrived. His outstanding athletic abilities were not to be exposed in a typical fashion. It seemed that Scott's aspirations were delayed, and he had been overlooked.

Scott decided to push back discouragement and tackle his disappointment with a decision to prepare for the dream even without the invitation. He designed his own rigorous workout with weight training and conditioning, including running the stadium steps regularly. Deep inside, he knew that God would one day put him in front of the right people.

His golden opportunity came unofficially through a series of events at the University of Illinois where he had played college football. This same campus is where he trained and kept himself in shape. Representatives of the National Football League were on campus and they took a closer look at him. His single focus on athletic preparation did not go to waste.

The NFL representatives were amazed at how physically fit Scott was, and they were equally impressed as they ran him through their workout. His forty-yard dash time was 4.24 seconds. For perspective, statistics reveal that since the Scouting Combine began measuring times electronically, no faster time exists. Scott finally had the attention of the NFL.

Scott joined the Washington Redskins in 1995. He enjoyed nine years in the NFL, balancing out his career with the San Diego Chargers and the Denver Broncos. Scott later became a state representative in Austin, Texas, representing the citizens of the 33rd district. Scott had a specific plan to work while delayed—but what if you don't have a plan?

Santina's husband had lost his job, causing her to wonder how their family would face the future. Delays and disappointments loomed everywhere. While waiting, her husband joyfully accepted a position as director at a local mission where he was paid poverty level wages. Santina prayed at her kitchen table and wondered what she could do to help.

Not many days later, her church received a phone call asking if they knew anyone who could do an in-store demonstration. They needed someone who had a great outgoing personality and a sense of salesmanship. The inquiry was passed on to Santina. The following weeks were spent learning the business. Santina took the initiative to meet with manufacturers, corporations and venders. Circumstances changed, and eventually the widowed owner of the company offered the entire business to Santina.

Her home-based business made its first million from Santina's kitchen table. Then it jumped to six million with offices and warehouses. Her question "What can I do?" was answered beyond her basic need as she met the needs of others. Santina brought all her family into the business.

The persistence of seeking till you find is often met with opportunities customized just for you.

A commercial pilot logged into his airline's upcoming flight schedule. He made a bid for a two-day job. All crew assignments were made based on availability and seniority. It was then that Peter Schreiber noticed a flight open for the leg from Boston to Los Angeles, so he bid on it. Normally, crewmembers pencil-in their names for a desired flight, then there is a thirty-minute window in which any other pilot with higher seniority may bump them.

The day before, Peter made arrangements for the flight and packed his bags. But the odd thing was, Peter never received the confirmation call. He assumed the delay in confirmation meant he had been bumped because the flight had been given to another pilot who outranked him.

During that fateful thirty-minute window, Tom McGuinness had bumped Peter so he could have the job. Consequently, Peter's request for Flight 11 was denied. The Boston to Los Angeles flight was scheduled to depart at 7:45 a.m. on September 11, 2001.

On that beautiful New England morning, the airliner pushed off from the gate on time. Once they had climbed to 23,000 feet, the autopilot engaged and Tom sat back to enjoy the flight. Nothing could have prepared him—or the world—for the course of events that took place that morning. Terrorists overtook Flight 11 as part of a concerted effort to attack New York's World Trade Center and the Pentagon. Flight 11 flew into the North Tower later that morning.

At first, Peter Schreiber did not even realize it was the very flight he had bid on until later in the day when people started calling him over and over. Days later, Peter returned to the American Airlines computer and tried again to log in for Flight 11 on September 11, 2001. Three words popped up on the screen that caught his emotions, "Sequence failed continuity." This coded message was used to denote flights that never reached their destination. Peter was gravely sobered that someone had voluntarily taken his seat. He said that later when he saw the burning hole where his seat would have been, it gave him a sense of urgency and obligation for how he wants to live today.

Delays of any kind and detours are part of life. Outcomes are yet to be determined.

A fourteen year old teenage boy accompanied his mother, grandmother, and sister on a camping trip in the mountains of Colorado. The purpose of the trip was to drop off his sister at a music camp while the rest of the family enjoyed time together. Work demanded the father stay behind, but he commissioned his son to oversee the family. His father reminded him that he was the man of the hour, and to take care of all the special women on the trip. They drove from Illinois to the Rocky Mountains in their car, pulling a pop-up tent camper.

After a week's stay, his sister was picked up and taken to the campsite to join the rest of her family. Everyone was exhausted and ready to head back home to Illinois. Ominous looking clouds were rolling in at a fast pace, and the mother thought they could beat the storm by a few hours if they broke camp immediately. She reasoned that starting the journey home in the late afternoon would give them a head start.

The plan was great for all the ladies, but, for some reason, the young son strongly disagreed. Jon was typically easy going, but he suddenly rose up in stubborn protest and said they were *not* going home now. His reason was that it would be too late in the day to start such a long trip. The mother and son continued to debate the issue, but the son was unbending. Finally, he laid down the trump card by saying, "Dad said *I* was the man in charge, and we are *not* going now." Since he was the only one who knew how to take down the camper, they ended up staying. His mother was irritated, and was even more upset when the downpour during the night soaked all their camping equipment. She dreaded the thought of packing it the next day. If only her son would just have listened to her.

The following morning, the campground was still muddy and the camping equipment was thoroughly soaked. Annoyed by the extra work their soggy delay had caused, the family of four started home. A short distance down the road they stopped for fuel. The mother wanted to confirm the best direction to enter the canyon for the quickest route home. The attendant told her that the canyon was closed and advised her of an alternate road she would need to take. Again, half-irritated, she now added this unexpected route to the list of reasons that proved they *should* have left the night before.

A little miffed, she asked, "Why is the canyon closed today?"

"Lady," the gruff attendant asked, "Don't you know what happened last night? The canyon flooded during the evening. Everyone who was traveling through it at the time was killed and washed away."

The mother was speechless as she thought back to the night before and calculated the time they would have traveled through the canyon. She quickly realized that their lives would have been lost in the raging current of the river. When her teenage son heard the story, he sat in quiet reflection, knowing that he had obeyed his father and had been given wisdom to care for the carload of special women in his charge.

This story holds deep significance to me because that stubborn son was my brother, Jon. The plan to protect and preserve our lives was cleverly disguised as an inconvenient delay. We later found out that ten to fourteen inches of rain fell in a very concentrated area and sent a rampaging wall of water through the Big Thompson Canyon, changing the course of the river and killing 143 people. It is considered Colorado's worst natural disaster.

Of course, not everyone's life is spared in life's unfolding mysteries. Every story does not have a happy ending. In a few of the stories I have recounted in this book some lives were tragically lost, and I do not take that lightly. Those losses are disturbingly unexplainable and are a personal source of sadness. A survivor sometimes experiences survivor's guilt when they wonder why they were saved and others lost. Too often, the answers are not clear. Yet, I believe survivors have an obligation to live life well in memory of those less fortunate. Delays, detours, and disappointments may cause you to adjust your plans and your attitudes; this is more evidence that you are not stuck.

Life is fragile and a big picture unfolds. Each day and its prospects must never be taken for granted. You're not stuck—you've been positioned.

CONFINEMENT

Do you have any phobias? I do. Mine is getting something stuck over my head. Though I know I can, in time, maneuver out of that uncomfortable place, it still causes me to panic. Nothing is more confining than feeling stuck. When fear is added to the equation the mounting pressure can feel unbearable.

One evening two of our daughters, Holly and Lydia, were in our large master closet, scavenging for some outfits among a section of my seasonal garments. There they discovered the dress I wore for their sister's wedding years before. They convinced me to try it on.

At first all seemed fun and games as the dress fit surprisingly well. Putting on the dress was easy, but taking it off was a nightmare. My arms got stuck and the bodice of the dress began to choke me. Unfortunately, my feelings of claustrophobia were perfectly synchronized with the girls' hysterical laughter. It did not help my predicament. Panic set in as I struggled desperately to get free. I was stuck with no one who would take me seriously. Eventually the girls helped me, though still laughing at my reaction. I escaped, but I was sweating profusely and determined to cut that beautiful dress into rags.

The struggle for freedom in many of life's situations is actually an important catalyst for development.

Tony and I were once part of a team outreach in a women's correctional facility in Pennsylvania. A talented group of singers, comedians, speakers, and a sound crew joined forces to encourage the incarcerated women. Our group made multiple presentations over two days. It was held in December and snow lay everywhere as we were escorted to the prison auditorium by armed guards. I started to feel ill about fifteen minutes before the inmates were expected to arrive. I'm not sure if it was nerves or low blood sugar, but I asked a female team member to go with me to the restroom. The guard escorted us to a door that was wedged open for the convenience of the team that otherwise was kept locked, due to prison protocol. However, when the door closed the wedge had inadvertently dislodged. The lock was on the outside and the guard had moved on. Immediately, a sense of panic set in for both of us.

My new friend, Anna, frantically pounded on the door, but there was no response. The more she pounded the more desperate she became. Realizing one of us needed to stay calm, I paced the floor while she cried for help. To calm my own growing panic I consoled myself that eventually someone would realize I was missing since I was one of the speakers.

After an uncomfortable amount of time had passed I walked over to the wall and felt its cold, concrete blocks. I discovered a welcomed bit of fresh air and immediately searched for its source. I found a small crack in the wall and pressed my nose into it in order to smell freedom. It helped calm my fears, as Anna relentlessly called for help. Soon, a prison guard freed us. I walked into the prison auditorium excited to see everyone—actually, to see *anyone*. The expectant audience of women made up for all of my anxieties. They were the best audience ever, laughing, crying, and singing. I knew I would never take my freedom for granted again.

Sometimes when you find yourself in a tight place, stuck and alone, you must apply resourcefulness. Just ask my mother.

One day after everyone had left the house, Mom decided to fix the dryer vent in our basement laundry area. She climbed up onto the dryer to reach behind it in hopes of reconnecting the hose. But she stretched too far and got stuck between the wall and the dryer, standing on her head. There was no one to help her get out. Trying not to panic, she could feel the blood rushing to her head. With little room in which to maneuver, Mom reached to the side of the dryer in search of anything she might use to wiggle her way up the wall. Thankfully, her hands latched onto something familiar: an old laundry stick my grandmother had often used with her antique wringer washer. Back in the old days, the stick was used to lift clothing out of hot, sudsy water before it went through the wringer. Mom had kept it. I doubt my grandmother ever considered the timely rescue this old stick would one day provide for her daughter. A piece of history gave my mom the leverage she needed to push her way up and over to freedom. In a pinch, resourcefulness and sheer determination can push us through to a safer place.

Yet, not all stories of confinement tell of a temporary status. Many times in our prevailing sense of panic we oddly settle for confinement. We are tempted to allow past failures to morph into passivity and unbelief. This kind of temptation intends for us to lose sight of creative problem solving. If we forget to apply the extra effort required to break free, the entrapping effects of old habits and deep rooted thought patterns will continue to hold us in their tight grasp.

Have you forgotten that you can help yourself reach for more? Settling never satisfies. Why not explore what you need to free yourself from, such as the recurring sense of limitations and narrow thinking? You may have to change your habits. You may have to shake up your daily routine. You may even have to struggle. Don't fear the notion of new possibilities. Don't fear what it takes to move on and move up. That is where you will find your higher sense of purpose.

Another December I came close to confinement in a revolving door of a beautiful hotel in downtown Atlanta. I was scheduled to speak at a national women's conference that evening. As I approached the entrance of the hotel I held the arm of my husband in one hand and in the other I juggled my purse and my carry-on. In my attempt to enter the revolving door my bag got caught in the motion. Fortunately, a quick tug was all that was required for my bag to rejoin me. While waiting for the door to finish its rotation, a life principle was etched onto my consciousness that is vivid to me and remains to this day.

Many choose to live life in confining, repetitive circumstances, not unlike taking up residency within a revolving door. There, they can view life moving all around them, which accentuates their ongoing predicament. From their fixed vantage point, they can see those close to them moving unencumbered to their destinations of choice. Behind the door people are walking on the sidewalk, enjoying unrestricted access to destinations unknown. Beyond the door are more people enjoying every opportunity that comes their way. Yet, there they stand, in their own isolated world, waiting. It only takes a few pushes to move toward the open area where opportunities abound. But they have to push.

Perhaps you need to push to finish your degree or change careers. Push to improve your skills. When you add increased value to any position it is often rewarded with promotion and financial increase. Push away from the table and return to a weight that feels good and is healthier. Push past your fears. Push past the thought that you are too young or too old to live your passion and dream. Push your constant working to the side and re-introduce yourself to your family. Push through the crowd of skeptics and find people who believe in you.

You still have room to push. You are not stuck. Push some more. You might ask, "What if I miss the window of opportunity and cannot make my entrance?" Then stay in the rotation. Your turn will come again. Just keep pushing. The biggest mistake is to stand still and do nothing. So push.

Then, push a little more!

A little boy once discovered a cocoon. He wondered if a butterfly had formed and if it was ready to come out of its tight quarters. The boy decided he would use his pocketknife to cut open the cocoon and help the butterfly escape. Unfortunately, this resulted in killing the beautiful creature. In order to live free the butterfly needed the struggle of breaking out of the cocoon. The butterfly's struggle to emerge as a new creature is a gift. It strengthens him for the days to come and for freedom's flight.

Likewise, our places of confinement may feel undesirable, yet something of beauty develops there. Do not begrudge the small places in life because they are merely temporary. Instead, embrace them as the birthplace of new discoveries and strength. A tight place creates a vantage point from which to gain fresh insights.

I walked with friends one day to the porch of our country home to bid them farewell. Once they were in their vehicle, I waved to them and said, "We're glad you came. Thanks for coming to see us."

Suddenly, the man turned to look at me and said, "Gail, I wish you could see what I see." I yelled back, "Tell me what you see."

"There's a whirlwind of hundreds of butterflies all around you. It's beautiful."

I promptly shouted, "The cocoon is open!"

Often the cocoons of our life have already opened and await us to take flight. Spread your wings and explore where they will take you. Courageously embrace the change. A metamorphosis, of any kind, is life changing and full of hope. Trust the process. You are not stuck. You are in transition to something better. Refuse the temptation to return to the cramped quarters you left behind. If the butterfly returned to his old cocoon he would discover maggots residing there, feasting on the leftovers of yesterday. The same is true in our lives whenever we slip back into old thought patterns and habits. Explore your newfound beauty and take flight to new possibilities.

The other familiar place of confinement is one which most have endured through natural childbirth. It is the confines of the human birth canal. Imagine a full-term baby refusing entrance into this tight passage. The birth canal seems too narrow with no wiggle room. The expectant mother on the other hand is eager to deliver her little one to a safe place so both can breathe with ease. Amazingly, a few of the benefits of passing through the birth canal include the fact that the pressure helps to expel amniotic fluid in the baby's lungs and nasal areas. The baby also receives protective bacteria that contribute to a healthy immune system. In addition, the passage helps stimulate the cardiovascular system.

Just beyond the narrow constraints of life's birth canal and of natural struggle awaits a harbor of unlimited potential and new life. That life—your life—is about expansion and increase. Don't fear the transition and what is strangely new or narrow. In time you will adapt. Your life is a continuum, so keep going. Keep pushing. Keep transitioning. You have more to discover. You have a finish line to cross. The winner's circle awaits you.

Do an inventory of your life and discern what constricts your talents and potential. You may discover that your limitations are self-imposed. Then design a plan of action that moves you toward your desired end, even if it begins with baby steps. You can shed what once confined you and taste new freedom.

Just PUSH! You're not stuck—you've been positioned.

Butler

I once heard it said that God will send you a butler who will open a door you could not see or unlock on your own. I believe I have been sent many in my life, and each has provided me with more than my heart could articulate. One such butler was my dear friend, Zig Ziglar.

I met Zig during the sunset years of his career and the beginning of mine. I was in the middle of a slow season in my life, after relocating to the Southwest from the Midwest. My talents were unused and my heart's desires denied. I felt overlooked and desperate for purpose. Finally, one winter morning I said to my husband, "Do you know what I would like to do this year?"

"What?" he replied casually.

"I want to speak for some corporations and have lunch with Zig Ziglar." Up to that time I had never spoken for any corporation, nor had I met Zig Ziglar personally. Unmoved by my lofty wish my husband simply said, "Okay," and went on to do his work.

Nine months later my audacious request became reality. During the fall I was invited to speak for several corporations. Each audience responded with enthusiasm. However, it all paled in comparison to the phone call I received near Thanksgiving.

"Is this Gail McWilliams?" It was an associate of Zig Ziglar. "My name is Bryan. Your name was given to me for consideration as a speaker for the Ziglar Corporation. Would you be willing to speak for us?" I suddenly stood up at my desk with a smile, although I did not trust what my ears heard. He continued, "We want to schedule you when Mr. Ziglar is in town. He will want to meet you."

Nearly one year to the day, when I had stated my heart's desire, I was at the front of the room with Mr. Ziglar in the front row. He had asked me to tell my story and speak to his staff for thirty minutes.

Little did we know my spoken request would change my life and set me on a course that has expanded into a super highway. I often wonder what would have developed if I had talked myself out of stating the impossible.

After speaking for twenty-nine minutes I turned the front of the room back over to Mr. Ziglar. He stood up and I sat down, but he said nothing. This awkward silence lasts for eternity when you cannot see. Finally, my husband leaned over and said, "Mr. Ziglar is crying." Later, Zig's assistant told my husband that it was only the second time in twenty years he had seen Mr. Ziglar cry publicly.

While others wiped tears from their eyes and the room fell silent, we waited for Zig to regain his composure. Finally he spoke. "I have never been more impacted by a life story." I could not believe what I heard. He continued with more words of encouragement and then stated emphatically, "Gail! You must write your story and tell the masses." I smiled and publicly received his encouragement, but privately, doubted the impact my story could have on anyone.

Mr. Ziglar was right. One year after Zig's directive, I finished my manuscript. I visited Zig to ask if he would consider writing the foreword, to which he said, "Absolutely."

During the first four months of its release, my autobiography was embraced by thousands of readers stateside and carried to sixty nations. I soon realized people related to a story of hope and triumph over tragedy. All of it confirmed the power of a life message.

Seeing Beyond, with a special foreword by Zig Ziglar, continues to impact lives and has been translated into Spanish. The title alone has placed me on a speaking circuit where I help others see beyond life's obstacles and challenges. The subtitle is now the motto at the end of each of my national radio features: "When you choose to look past the horizon, the sky's the limit."

Interestingly, back when I mentioned I wanted to have lunch with Zig Ziglar, I had never read any of his books or attended any of his seminars. I simply knew him as the icon of motivation, and this was the direction my heart was growing. I heard of his infectious encouragement and knew people were impacted by his life to move forward with their own. Beyond Mr. Ziglar's ability to motivate, he always stood firm in his faith in God and his love for people. Zig Ziglar was a breath of fresh air to corporate America. I wanted to be the same.

Since my first encounter with the legend of motivation I have had the joy to share several lunches with my dear friend. Each encounter has been a defining moment in my life, so I have threaded them throughout this book. He is more than just a man of positive attitude and success. He is one who spoke to the destiny within my own life and encouraged me to reach for more. The path you are currently walking on may appear to lead to a dead end, but your view is limited. When you feel stuck, a butler may be just what you need.

One fall I was asked to speak to a group of national leaders in Washington D.C. I would be the first speaker on the program, and my message was to set the tone for a call to live with vision. At the end of the event a gentleman in the audience said that after the first two sentences were out of my mouth he decided to invite me to speak at Liberty University, the largest Christian university in the world.

Months later I stood before ten thousand college students in a basketball arena while thousands more watched on the Internet.

What a joy and an honor to pour vision into the next generation of leaders, calling them to live their dream with passion.

From that same Washington D.C. event I was asked to do an hour-long national radio interview with a woman I had admired for years. I had always wanted to meet this intelligent and articulate lady but never dreamed we would be fast friends as we teamed together to encourage our beloved nation. One small door opened and became a domino effect for more.

Seated on a patio one evening at a resort outside of Las Vegas, another butler opened a door for me. Earlier in the day I had spoken at a leadership conference. I was enjoying the dry heat of the evening air and the beautiful starlit sky. Seated at a table next to my husband and me, a man was enjoying the same with his wife. I admired the gentleman's British accent and overheard snippets of his conversation. My curiosity got the best of me and I inquired, "Excuse me sir. Could you please tell me more about the information I just overheard?"

As we exchanged light conversation, I asked if he was attending the conference at the resort. He was not, but asked about me. I told him I was one of the speakers. My husband told me later that my new friend sat up straight and leaned in. However, I only heard his curiosity and intrigue when he asked, "Are you a corporate speaker?"

Our small talk turned into an intensely interesting conversation, including the exchange of phone numbers and email addresses. The British gentleman was an executive producer who was looking for speakers for large conventions. His last words to me that night were, "I look forward to your calling me."

Speak aloud your heart's desires and write them down. Take courage and be proactive. If you are waiting, then prepare. While you wait beware of sabotaging attitudes that could take hold. I have heard it said that boredom is an attitude. I think feeling stuck is a negative attitude as well. Waiting does not mean you are stuck.

You're just using times of transition to fully prepare. Be expectant and anticipate. A "butler" is about to open a door of opportunity beyond anything you could see or imagine.

When my radio feature was first conceived I attended a large media conference. The verdict was still out as to whether or not my broadcasts would draw a substantial audience. At that conference I met many "butlers" in passing. It was a bit overwhelming. Finally, it was my turn to spend an hour one-on-one with an influential media strategist. I asked pointedly, "Who would be important for me to meet?"

The strategist's answer was as thorough as it was discouraging. She named the top lawyer who worked exclusively with booking agents. She remarked, "Though he would be at the top of the list for you to meet, it is impossible. He is already booked for every day of the convention. He's unreachable."

Listening intently I asked, "What is his name again?"

Our strategy meeting over coffee came to an end after the designated hour. I thanked her for her input. As it happened, during the course of the convention I met several people on the list she gave me. All of them were important network connections. Later in the evening I was waiting with my husband to see the premier showing of a feature film at the convention. My husband forgot something in our hotel room, and we agreed I would wait while he went back to the room. I stood alone in a hallway of this magnificent Nashville resort.

I overheard two gentlemen in a friendly conversation who had come to stand near me. I could not help but hear the man's name. Amazingly, it was the *busy, unreachable* lawyer the strategist mentioned earlier that day. I waited for an appropriate time, then asked, "Excuse me. Are you…?" He moved closer to me and affirmed my hunch. I continued, "Sir, your name is valued above most and your work is celebrated by those who admire you. It is my joy to meet you. Do you have a minute?"

We stood and talked for over thirty minutes. His free advice was priceless and his sincere interest in my conceptual radio ideas encouraged me greatly. He introduced me to others and the network connections rippled. He thanked me and told me I had personally encouraged him as well.

You may feel locked out of your dreams and purpose for a season, but there is a "butler" who holds a key to a door you did not know existed. Prepare now to advance through the door when it is opened. Get ready to cross that threshold. Do not talk yourself out of what others call impossible. It is nonsense. When you seek, there are dreams to find. When you ask, there are answers to discover. Don't be surprised who is on the other side of the door. It may be better than you imagined. Just keep knocking.

Look for the butler who waits to open a door. Keep moving forward and watch for inexplicable surprises. You're not stuck—you've been positioned.

MIDNIGHT

At midnight on New Year's Eve in New York City, while crowds cheer and millions watch by television, the historic ball drops in Times Square. The passage from one year to a new one is welcomed with expectation of a fresh start and better days to come.

The idea for the ball originated with Adolph Ochs who purchased the struggling New York Times in 1896. His goal was to make the newspaper the number one publication in all of New York. The newspaper was headquartered in the middle of Manhattan in what would later be renamed Times Square. Ochs wanted something elaborate to draw attention to his new building and his growing business. He concocted a new way for New Yorkers to celebrate New Year's Eve in style, featuring glorious lights that weren't reliant upon fireworks.

Since the early 1900's the ball has had different designs. In 1907, Ochs commissioned the building of an electrically lit ball, which would be lowered on the flagpole of the roof of One Times Square (the new name of the newspaper's corporate headquarters). Ochs constructed his "New Year's Eve Ball" of iron and wood, adorned with one hundred 25-watt light bulbs. The ball was five feet in diameter and weighed 700 pounds. The ball was first lowered at the start of the 1908 New Year's celebration and became a yearly tradition.

In December of 1999 the dawn of a new millennium called for a newly designed ball. It was outfitted with spinning mirrors, 504 Waterford Crystals, and 168 halogen bulbs. Its finished weight tipped the scales at over 1,070 pounds.

Today, the ball is twelve feet in diameter, more than double its original 1907 size. It weighs in at over five metric tons and features LEDs and computerized lighting patterns. What an extravagant effort to celebrate the midnight watch each New Year's Eve.

Your own midnight hour may not have millions who cheer and watch your changes, but there is still something in motion that will play out in time.

Midnight hangs between the previous and what is yet to come. Unfortunately, it can be unsettling, isolated, and dramatic. Just ask Cinderella. Her midnight hour interrupted a dream come true and a dance with her charming Prince. Panic, loss, and disappointment added to the drama when Cinderella raced away as the clock struck midnight. She had not yet read the end of her own fairy tale and the royal changes that were to come. Perhaps your midnight crisis is similar. However, more is evolving than you may realize.

Obviously, your life and mine are about more than mere fairy tales and sugarcoated endings. The disappointment of goals unmet and pre-planned life agendas interrupted can be drastically disconcerting. The midnight crisis of sickness, tragedy, and death are never on anyone's calendar. Divorce, bankruptcy, and demotions tempt one to bolt, like Cinderella, to anywhere but where you are now. Feelings of entrapment cause you to think your midnight is relentless and unending. But what if you positioned yourself for new ideas, innovative strategies, and probing wisdoms? What if you believed that something good could come from all of it?

Midnights are not designed to be terminal, just transitional. The midnight hour is never a complete blackout. It is the unlit gateway to something brand new.

Stay the course and anticipate the dawn of something beyond your wildest dreams.

One June, everyone in our family went on vacation to the big skies of Montana. We still talk about it, and no trip has compared since. We were surrounded by snowcapped mountains in a cabin along a raging river.

One particular night involved only the guys. Long after everyone else went to bed, they decided to sit around the fire pit and talk. The backdrop of the starlit covering against the darkest midnight sky was undeniably a marvel, especially for city boys who rarely look up to see anything but streetlights and skylines. Constellations like the Big Dipper, visible satellites, and shooting stars enhanced the fireside chat. Thick clouds initially interrupted the view of the sky but soon moved out. While talking, our son noticed something out of the corner of his eye. He described it like a bright light coming over the hill headed towards them with a brilliance that was nearly blinding. It emerged above the mountain treetops and seemed to settle just above the mountain peaks. This incredible full moon brightly lit the whole area. The early morning surprise gave them a new view of nearby deer, surrounding acreage, and the swift white water river. The dark black sky had gradually transitioned to deep midnight blue. New hues and subtle shades were now evident. Then the large lunar impact gave way to the golden glimpse of the new morning sun. Within moments the darkness of the night had changed while the earth revolved and the new day announced its arrival.

I believe the same is true in our lives. The cloud cover of discouragement prevents us from resting in hope while dark personal midnights loom large in our minds. Consequently, we focus on the hopelessness of present circumstances and even build entire belief systems around disappointments and disillusionments. But what if there is more?

No matter your midnights, you can be confident that there is more than you can see in your dark hour, and there is promise of a bright day coming. Wait in expectant hope.

Do not despair. Your own epic story is not yet fully written. A single minute after midnight might be your first step toward better days ahead. Receive the comfort of an ancient warrior and king who said, "Weeping may last for the night, but joy comes in the morning."

Midnight transitions can come at any time on the clock. One from my life was on May 17, 2011. Our second grandson was born ten days early, at the top of the hour. Near the end of the same hour our festive joy drastically turned, and my family faced a dark midnight season that had little hope of earthly dawn.

After waiting with great anticipation for the expected new grand joy, we were finally able to hold the adorable blond-headed boy. Moments later, I received a devastating phone call. My mother was crying as she explained with fear in her voice, "I am at the hospital. Your dad has to have emergency heart surgery. It's serious."

I handed my new grandson, Oliver, back to the arms of his mother and leaned over to kiss my daughter on the cheek. I whispered, "I'm so sorry. I have to go." I was torn between the dawn of life and the midnight shadows of death.

I quickly left the downtown Baylor Hospital to hurry to the north Baylor Heart Hospital to be with my parents. It was Dad's 77th birthday and now life suddenly seemed so momentary. None of us were ready to say goodbye to our beloved patriarch. Dad's weakened heart was operating at seventeen percent of its normal capacity. It needed immediate attention. He was added to the list of surgeries for the following day. The long night was filled with visitors who came to comfort our family and pray for my dad. Once the word was out that my dad's life hung in the balance, visitors came from everywhere.

The recommended quadruple bypass was risky. I remember the surgeon coming to talk to the family about my Dad's prognosis. The anesthesiologist took Mom's hand and said, "We will do everything that we can, but your husband is a very, very sick man." Though we could not see the path, we did not face the midnight crisis alone. I remembered some comforting words from Psalms 23, "Though I walk through the valley of the shadow of death—You are with me."

At 1:30 p.m. the next day, under the steerage of his nurses, Dad embarked on a speedy wheelchair ride to the operating room where the surgeon waited. At 4:00 p.m. we heard the good news that the surgery went well. Time would tell. The medical condition referred to as "the widow maker" missed its victim this time.

Dad's recovery process was slow. His pain level combined with his rehab, were often difficult to bear, yet Dad persevered. The bright sunrise of the joyful birth of his little birthday buddy, his great grandson, Oliver, was a bright spot as Dad fought for every breath.

I am a firm believer that when you face death you will suddenly know how to live. Conversely, I also believe that how you have lived will help you face death. Dad continues to show me that in the middle of my darkest hour I can still have purpose, and each day dawns with renewed reasons to influence others for good.

Within six months of his surgery, Dad learned to leverage his decreased mobility to better position himself; he simply sat down at the computer and began to write. Since that tentative beginning, Dad has published four books, each filled with the gift of his teachings.

Dad is currently writing two more books. He writes for young leaders who need a word of encouragement and a seasoned mentor. In spite of health challenges and his need to live life at a slower pace, Dad chooses to invest in the lives of others. He delights in giving away dozens of books as an effort to encourage the next generation.

These past four years I have studied the effect that Dad's life continues to have on others. Even in the midst of his illness he is determined to focus on others. Dad determined that surviving that risky surgery was the only proof he needed that God had more for him to do. Faith in a living God makes all the difference in any midnight hour. Even if death had come, my Dad was prepared for an eternal dawn. Thankfully, this midnight did not prove fatal. I am grateful for the extra time we have had together.

However, many of our midnights are not life or death, but are points from which we make life-changing shifts or flex with new developments. It is reasonable to expect that in spite of the darkness, a life lesson will be learned or a new opportunity will appear.

America has faced the uncertainty of many midnight hours. Countless lives have been lost and innumerable injuries have been sustained to fight for an exceptional country with liberty and justice for all. Though America was established in 1776, the demoralized British sought revenge. They continued to battle the Americans for nearly another forty years. It was during this troubled time that British soldiers set the White House on fire, and planned to seize one of the most populated cities of that day, Baltimore, Maryland. But Fort McHenry would have to be taken first.

As the British were planning to attack the fort, two brave Americans rowed out into the Baltimore Bay with a white flag of truce, hoping to negotiate the release of a prisoner held on a British ship. The Americans were Francis Scott Key and John S. Skinner. They set sail from Baltimore to the British ship, HMS Minden. Their objective was to secure the release of Dr. William Beans, the elderly and beloved town physician of Upper Marlboro, who had been kidnapped from his home by the British. Dr. Beans was a personal friend of Mr. Key, and Skinner was a negotiator.

Multiple letters urging negotiations to release the prisoner were brought from British soldiers whose wounds had been treated by the doctor. The two men met with the British officers for one full week, and finally they agreed to release the elderly prisoner. Their success was delayed though, because now the ships were attacking Fort McHenry. Key and Skinner were now prisoners themselves, in effect, held captive like the prisoner they came to free.

Fort McHenry housed one thousand men, and the large British ships fired upon it relentlessly. Key prayerfully paced back and forth on the deck of the ship during the night, straining to see the flag that flew in the midst of the cannon fire. After all the fighting ceased, the flag that flew over the fort would announce the victor. The dark night was lit with the flames of warfare and persistent attacks. The night sky was sporadically illuminated with cannon fire, and a thick haze loomed over the water, preventing Francis Key from seeing what flag flew above the fort. At the break of dawn, he saw a thirty by forty-two foot American flag, with stripes and stars still flying triumphantly over the fort.

Francis Scott Key, inspired with a heart of gratitude, wrote our beloved national anthem, *The Star Spangled Banner,* after the midnight crisis ended and the dawn of a new day declared the victory.

Perhaps you feel stuck in a battle of your own. But what if midnight is the turnaround as you head to a new dawn? Stay centered in the kind of hope that sees beyond each storm and battle. Focus on a new horizon. One minute past midnight begins the dawning of a new day and leans all clocks in the direction of change.

You may have experienced too many midnight hours when you were surrounded in the darkness of your soul, unable to find your way. If you're not careful, life's disappointments will lead you to become cynical about your own dreams.

Personally, I have found hidden treasures in some of the darkest places of my life. I've learned that even overwhelming darkness brightens in time, when it is met head on with purpose and vision. I've learned to embrace the lessons and experiences of midnight as gifts that better enable me to shine as a light on the path of others. Midnight really does represent the turning point of a new day, a pivotal catalyst of hope with a new promise yet to dawn.

The light of dawn is the evidence that no midnight is dark enough to quench a sense of promise. You're not stuck—you've been positioned.

CRUCIBLE

Lunch or dinner engagements are frequently coupled with my speaking career. I love to ask people to tell me something about themselves I don't already know. Of course, it could be almost anything since I have only just met them. The fun is to surprise the others at the table with the hidden treasures of their colleagues' stories.

During one such luncheon my favorite icebreaker revealed some jaw-dropping bits of trivia. Of the eight executive team members who sat at our table, three of them burned down their houses as young boys, yet none of them was an arsonist. In all three instances the house fires were the results of accidents, each with strangely wild circumstances. While I listened I had a sudden urge to blow out the candles on the table. Hearing the stories of the unfortunate infernos accidentally started by those little boys caused me to remember two sets of personal friends who also survived house fires.

Leslie and Bob are equestrians who, along with two daughters, traveled the rodeo circuit. On this particular evening the road-weary quartet returned to their Florida home around one o'clock in the morning. Their daughters unloaded the horse trailer and led the horses to their stalls in the barn. Bob attended to some equipment in his machine shop while Leslie checked on the rest of the family, most of whom had retired hours earlier.

Bob was just falling into a twilight sleep when he heard a noise in the attic overhead that sounded like a *swoop*. He grabbed Leslie's arm and exclaimed, "I think the house is on fire!" Suddenly, aware of smoke coming from their bedroom ceiling they jumped to their feet. Leslie ran to her mother's room, opened the boys' bedroom doors along the way, and yelled, *"Get out! The house is on fire!"*

Bob ran to the girls' room and did the same. They could hardly see as they felt their way down the hallway in front of them. Leslie and her disoriented mother were the last to exit the house. Just as they ran down the driveway the windows of the house blew out. Leslie was sure glass shards would be imbedded in their backs.

Within minutes the roof collapsed. The attending firemen were amazed that the entire household escaped safely from such a fast-burning fire. Even the family dog caught up with them on the run. The alarming ordeal—from the initial sound of the ominous *swoop* to their house reduced to ashes and ruin—took a total of ten minutes.

All that physically remained of their house easily fit into one lone bucket. Yet this loss of a lifetime filled them with an abiding gratitude that they had everything they needed to rebuild a happy home—they had each other. Houses can be rebuilt, but lives are irreplaceable.

Kami and Clint had recently learned they were to become parents. It was Thanksgiving time and they had just returned home from the airport where they picked up friends. At the end of the day they parked their car in the garage and went inside.

Not too long after getting home Clint heard a noise that sounded like his water heater in the garage. He went out to open his garage door and heard a hissing sound. He also smelled radiator coolant. It was soon evident there was a small fire. He immediately called the fire department. Though the fire station was only one block from their house, the fire engine was in the holiday parade. Clint ended up making two emergency phone calls for help, but nearly one hour passed from his initial call before the fire truck arrived.

At first the fire seemed contained to the garage. But as it burned hotter it melted the coils of the attic door above and dropped the attic ladder into the garage. Fire relies on oxygen to build its speed and ferocity, and the down draft of the attic provided plenty. Within seconds the entire top of the house was ablaze. The unbelievably sad timing is that the fire truck finally rounded the corner onto their street just in time to watch it all go up in flames.

A small town atmosphere had compounded the effects of the ensuing disaster and needlessly contributed a circus-like chain of events. Unfortunately, it would be another two weeks before the couple received in the mail the recall notice for their car's cruise control, the mechanical culprit behind the cause of the fire.

Victims of fires are mercilessly stripped of everything they once held dear. Yet, in the aftermath of such devastating loss, they shared a precious blessing: their priorities were redefined overnight.

On Sunday, October 8, 1871, Chicago was ablaze with a raging fire that burned for two days. The legendary cause of this epic disaster is attributed to a cow knocking over a lantern in a barn. Witnesses indicate differently, but all confirm the same location in the devastated city for the fire's origin. Fear and loss spread as fast as the flames raged through Chicago's clapboard landscape. This endless supply of wooden buildings fueled the inferno, aided by a gusty, harsh, northeastern wind. When the last embers cooled, the face and people of Chicago were changed forever.

Chicago experienced a sort of Renaissance due to that fire. After its reconstruction Chicago became one of the most populated and economically driven cities in America. The fire, it seems, was the catalyst that bonded the citizens of the city together and resulted in the impassioned reconstruction of their cherished city.

One late fall I had the pleasure of speaking before the dedicated employees of Eagle Bronze, Inc., a Wyoming-based company that produces magnificent bronze monuments. Their most famous work is displayed in Dallas where the world's largest continuous bronze theme is on display. It features a herd of fifty-nine bronze cattle positioned on a grassy knoll in the heart of the city. It was created as a tribute to the historic cattle drives of the Southwest. This renowned foundry also produced The Equestrian, the three-story statue that is featured at the entrance to the El Paso International Airport, as well as the six large bronze panther statues for the Carolina Panthers of the National Football League.

Hours before the time came for me to speak to their crew, I asked to have a tour of their foundry. Each department's role in the creative process is critical to the successful outcome of the final product. The wonder of it all starts with an unassuming lump of clay, strategically positioned in the hands of an artist.

Once the foundry receives the artist's clay sculpture, it is precisely measured and photographed in detail. It is crucial that every minute element is captured and recorded because the next step is deconstruction, where the clay sculpture is systematically sliced and reduced to manageable parts. These individual pieces are coated with multiple layers of silicone or latex. The molds are then encased in plaster for support, much like an exoskeleton. What remains is a negative impression, the inside-out version of the desired end product.

This mold has hot molten wax repeatedly poured into it. The wax is swished thoroughly around the mold's interior cavity and then poured back out until the wax builds up sufficiently inside the mold. Artisans continually reference the recorded measurements and photos taken earlier to assure every detail of the original is captured.

After technicians add channels through which liquid bronze will travel to every nook and cranny of the mold, it heads into the shell room where the pieces are repeatedly dunked into ceramic slurry and coated with sand. This shell material coats the artwork inside and out, completely encasing the wax, but leaving one small opening. These multiple layers harden and form a heat-tolerant coating.

Next, they are placed in a furnace heated to 1,600°F, where the encased wax sculpture is completely melted and drained out. What is left behind is a hardened ceramic mold, which can withstand the fire to come. Now comes the crucible. This is a special pot in which the bronze ore is melted. The bronze pourers are attired in special heat-resistant clothing, including gloves and facemasks. The crucible and the bronze ore are heated to 2,300°F. While the bronze is melting the shell molds are gradually reheated to 1,600°F. If not pre-heated the ceramic molds would crack under the heat of the bronze. Molten metal enthusiasts refer to this as thermal displacement.

As the intensity builds, the two men must screen everything perfectly. The bronze continues to melt while the pourers monitor its temperature. Dross and waste periodically rise to the top of the molten bronze and are carefully ladled off. If not removed they could undermine the integrity of the bronze.

At precisely the right moment the pourers remove the pre-heated shell molds from the furnace and place them upside down in a pit. Using vice-like grips, the pourers carefully carry the crucible full of molten bronze to the pit where they meticulously pour the lava-like liquid into the molds. This must be done as quickly as possible because the bronze begins to rapidly cool the moment it leaves the heat. Within an hour it will be cool to the touch.

Tears fell down the sides of my face as I watched this incredible part of the casting process. So much of my life had been formed in the crucible of trials and loss. I could not stop the tears as I looked on. There was reassurance in learning that the purpose of the fire of the crucible is to preserve, not to destroy. It merely refines. I was comforted to know highly skilled hands set the fire at the right temperature. But *nothing* prepared me for what came next.

After the newly cast bronze pieces completely cooled, the workers hoisted them over their heads and hurled them into a bed of shell. This begins the cracking process. The workers are very careful not to mar the surface of the sculpture as the remaining shell is removed. In disbelief, I was almost offended. *Hadn't the fire been enough?* I spoke up and asked my tour guide, "Why are the pieces handled with such harshness?"

She explained that the molds must be entirely broken away from the newly formed bronze pieces. Until this step is complete the bronze has precious little value. What emerged in the rubble and debris of their broken outer shells were all the newly cast bronze components. These were all necessary to finally fashion the lasting monument envisioned by the artist, when all he first had to work with was soft clay.

In that moment I saw a truth about sustainable leadership. After enduring an intense trial by fire, most of us assume we will never experience a similar hardship again. Having survived the worst life could offer, we wrongly feel inoculated to future calamities. Yet, situations continue to come our way, tempting us to lose heart or become offended by a misunderstanding or another's harsh or rough treatment. Taking a last stab at self-preservation, it is only natural for us to want to proclaim, "Enough!" I wondered, aren't those added offenses merely heavy-handed distractions tempting us to give up and walk away? We must not abandon our passionate quests. The glorious end is almost in sight.

The final touches on the sculpture begin with sand blasting to remove any foreign particles that remain. Then, through the processes of welding, grinding and buffing, the individual parts are rejoined to become a whole. At long last it becomes an exquisite piece of art, touched by the hands of no fewer than a dozen skilled craftsmen and talented artists. The result is a durable monument that will impact generations to come.

If you and I withstand the assembly line of life and its fiery trials, we are merely freed of an outer shell. However, what results is a masterpiece and a monumental legacy we leave behind. Life can get heated, but a process is underway that removes the unwanted and establishes an enduring foundation. You're not stuck—you've been positioned.

PUZZLED

Have you ever been stuck with some unanswered questions from life that simply did not make sense? Even when our view is skewed and dim, the totality of life *must* be about more than we can see with the naked eye. But, how do you position yourself to understand the unexplainable?

My mother came to help us out for a day as we moved into a new house. We worked all afternoon side by side. We all remarked how energetic Mom was for her seventy-three years and how she could work circles around the rest of us. Mom started to leave early in the evening, but I persisted in asking her to stay and join us for our first dinner in the new house. I remember well the fun conversation and all the laughter around our table that night. Hugging each other as she was leaving, we agreed how much fun work can be with someone by your side.

After a thirty minute drive home my mom entered the complex where she and my dad were living at the time. She thought it odd the security gate was wide open when it should have been closed. She called my dad on the cell phone as a precaution. "I'm here. Would you mind coming to escort me in?" He quickly replied, "Sure. Let me get my shoes on and I'll be right there."

It was approximately ten o'clock at night, and she had parked near a large light. Intending to meet him halfway, she opened her car door. Startled, she met the eyes of a stranger whose heart was set on evil. Within seconds, my mother was attacked and thrown to the ground. The attacker relentlessly hit her blow after blow. Raising up to resist his strength, she was hurled to the ground once more. During the assault she had great presence of mind to sound her car alarm. People came running from all directions and even watched from their windows, but could not come to her aid in time.

As my dad bent over Mom lying on the pavement, the assailant sped away in their car. My dad thought they both would be run over. The thug easily exited the complex unhindered through the disabled security gate.

Dad frantically aided his wife of fifty-three years, not knowing if she was going to live or die. Within minutes we were called and we immediately rushed to the hospital emergency room. My young-hearted, vivacious mother, now unable to move, looked as if she had aged twenty-five years in the span of one night. She lay in excruciating pain, deeply bruised, and with her back broken in two places. With her life hanging in the balance, Dad stood at the side of his bride as the emergency room staff skillfully cared for her.

With a trembling, traumatized voice, Mom softly said, "I forgive the man who did this to me." More astounding were her next words. "Gail, you must go on with your speaking engagement this week." In spite of the trauma she was mindful of an important upcoming speaking event. I shook my head and resisted; tears falling from my eyes, saying, "No, I cannot go." She softly insisted, "You must." Slowly continuing, she struggled to talk, but bravely added, "This is only a distraction to keep you from touching other lives."

Her words from the heart in a time of crisis were proof of a life lived by prioritizing godly purposes above her own. The issues of forgiveness first sprang like a fountain of life in the middle of reprehensible horror. Her heart was securely rooted in a lifetime of faith.

Offenses will come into our lives. How we deal with them is our choice. Choosing forgiveness opens the heart to true wholeness.

An expectant young couple from Colorado anticipated the birth of their new daughter. The baby was active and playful in the womb. Each month the mother bonded more with her little girl in anticipation of her birth. But then she and her husband had to face shocking news. Due to a rare condition, their baby had no chance of survival.

Upon taking its first breath the newborn would die instantly. The unborn baby was diagnosed with a rare condition in which the infant's brain is grossly undeveloped. They faced a decision with no chance of a happy ending. Each day was more painful than the previous one. The medical professionals were suggesting she terminate her pregnancy in hopes of alleviating any elongated pain for the family.

Laura chose to keep her baby but the next few weeks were dark. She decided to treat her little girl like the previous pregnancies of their other healthy children. Warnings concerning her decision freed the doctor of any medical liability and left Laura and her family to sort out their emotions, bolster their hearts, and plan for the agonizing day of delivery. Laura hoped for a miracle, yet dealt courageously with the feared reality.

They named their precious little one Pearl. Each day was planned with loving thoughtfulness to enjoy the tender moments they had left with their little bundle, tucked away in safety for now. Laura would swing at the playground for Pearl to enjoy. She and her husband traveled to Ireland to give Pearl a taste of the world. Group family hugs and dances were common as everyone tried to put their arms around Baby Pearl still in the womb.

Fear waited for Laura in the night, filled with her tears and the impossible questions of her heart. She tried to hope, yet dared not to. Pearl continued to grow in her while Laura prepared for the first glimpse of her little girl.

Toward the end of her pregnancy complications started with Laura. Her belly was extended like a mother carrying full-term twins. Excess amniotic fluid was building up sending her to the emergency room where it was removed three liters at a time.

One day while they drained the excess fluids Laura's water broke. The seriousness of each minute heightened the alarm of the medical team scurrying to now care for both patients in jeopardy. With monitors everywhere Laura could hear the beating of Pearl's heart slowing down. Familiar with the labor and delivery procedures, Laura said, "Take me off the monitor. I do not want to hear my baby slowly die."

Instantly, a near death complication occurred. Laura started hemorrhaging severely. The critical blood loss could not be stopped. "I must take the baby and possibly your uterus by Caesarian immediately," cried the distressed physician. Suddenly, within seconds, Laura's bleeding completely stopped. In amazement, the surgical staff fell silent.

With a stern directive, the doctor exclaimed, "Quickly, get me a monitor to see what's happening inside Laura." While the delivery team watched in awe via ultrasound, they saw a little baby with an undeveloped brain use her head. She wedged herself in a cavity opened where the placenta had torn away from the uterine wall. Stunned by the turn of events, the medical team watched the tender moment of Pearl intuitively positioning herself to save her mommy's life. Amazingly, Pearl stayed tucked in the gaping tear for over 24 hours.

The doctor announced his plans for a Caesarian section to remove Pearl from her mother due to the delay in Pearl's arrival. The next day brought a tender farewell. At 5:00 a.m. Laura lovingly whispered to her little one, "It's okay if you come now. Mommy will be fine." With full permission and her lifesaving task accomplished, Pearl at last entered the birth canal to face death as she was born naturally.

The midnight sorrow, coupled with the dawn of a new day, brought Laura and her family to a place they had never known. Their treasured little Pearl still increases in value to this day. Pearl saved her mommy's life and uterus, allowing Laura to get pregnant again and give birth to Pearl's little sister, Lucy.

Laura and her husband have fittingly named their organization "String of Pearls." Their dream is to establish a house where they will host families who face the same dark hour, offering a bright spot of refuge and understanding. They are currently raising funds to establish the House of Pearl. Their ultimate prayer and hope was a miracle at birth, which would prove the fatal diagnosis wrong. A miracle did come, but in a way no one ever imagined.

The purpose of such an experience is a mystery. We expect a long life for each birth. Some live a long life and touch no one, while others lose their lives too soon, but touch everyone. The definition of a hero is one who lays down his or her life for another. When you suffer a great loss the challenge is not to become embittered, though your life will never be the same. Managing the loss, pain, and heartache is key since the heart never forgets. Just surviving a loss is remarkable, but turning it for good is amazing grace. Use your loss to help others. The empathy and compassion offered to someone in their midnight crisis is better received from another who has passed through the same dark hour.

Tragedies often birth opportunities to help others. Take for instance, some of my friends:

Rebekah, after the stillbirth of her son, started a support organization to help families who have lost babies due to miscarriage, stillbirth, or early infant death. It is called MEND (Mommies Enduring Neonatal Death).

Tracey heads up a water safety vest campaign, for families who love the beach, in honor of her three-year-old grandson, Wyatt, who tragically drowned in a lake. Water safety classes and life vests are provided each summer, compliments of Remembering Wyatt Dale Water Safety Awareness, a non-profit organization.

Jay Dan started an after prison care program. Forgiven Felons provides housing, clothing, hygiene, job search assistance, and spiritual training. He saw this need while he was still in prison. He watched friends of his get out of prison, but were back in again before Jay Dan even made parole. He told God he would do anything to help men stay out. This need was underscored when Jay Dan was repeatedly rejected for management jobs because of his felony. So he started his own business, which helps these men with part-time work.

Former Navy SEAL, Dave Roever, mobilizes his organization, Operation Warrior RECONnect, to rebuild the wounded soldier in soul and mind when they return from their time of service. He suffered his own devastating personal loss when a white phosphorous grenade exploded in his hand during combat in Vietnam.

Joni Eareckson Tada had a diving accident as a teen and is one of the longest living quadriplegics. Her organization, Joni and Friends, aids the disabled with a plethora of programs including wheelchair provision, family retreats, television and radio, public awareness of medical issues, international outreach, and construction to address access for the disabled.

Countless stories like these reflect people who turned their loss into gain. You're not stuck in tragedy but positioned to help others—because you better understand their pain.

Horatio G. Spafford once penned the famous lyrics to the soul-stirring hymn of yesteryear entitled, "It is Well with My Soul." Horatio and his wife, Anna, had four daughters. They lived in Chicago where he was a successful businessman and lawyer. Spafford had invested heavily in real estate holdings north of the expanding city of Chicago in 1871. Later that same year, the Great Fire of Chicago destroyed this sizeable investment.

In 1873, with a concern for his wife's health, he planned a holiday in England. A pressing business matter at the last minute demanded he stay behind. He arranged to follow his family in a few days. On November 22nd the ship the family traveled on, the S.S. Ville du Havre, was struck by the Lutheran, an English vessel, and sank in twelve minutes. Mrs. Spafford survived and cabled her husband from Wales, "Saved alone." Spafford left immediately to join his wife. During the voyage his ship approached the area of the ocean thought to be the place the ship carrying his four daughters had sunk. There he penned the words to "It is Well with My Soul."

Spafford was a devout Christian and his unshakeable faith positioned him to endure his storms and loss in spite of the tears, sorrow, questions, and survivor's guilt. Spafford wrote, *"When peace like a river attendeth my way, when sorrows like sea billows roll; whatever my lot, thou hast taught me to say, 'It is well, it is well with my soul.' "*

No doubt, there are things in life that do not make sense. I made a decision long ago not to spend all my energy on what I could not understand, but instead give my focus to that which I know. My soul is anchored while I wait. I know it may not be easy and the heart knows its own sorrow, but you may have to decide whether you are stuck in unanswered questions—or positioned to use your heartache to help others.

Your limited scope about life's perplexities does not mean there is not a bigger picture yet to be discovered. You're not stuck—you've been positioned.

IMPRINTED

I continue on this uncharted course of diminished eyesight and am learning how to maneuver in the hazy places of life. Many ask what I can physically see. This is hard to explain since each day my vision vacillates from a little to less; and without notice, it often diminishes from blurry to mere shadows. But, seeing is something I practice no matter the view. I truly am your best friend because you always look great to me.

I had the advantage of having great eyesight for the first two decades of my life. My vision was in no danger until I became pregnant with our first child. With each subsequent pregnancy I lost more eyesight—yet, my *vision* has remained intact.

I have always had a vivid imagination. My world has advantages since I can imagine beyond the worst perspectives. I am not as easily distracted as a sighted person because I remain focused on vision. When you have vision you can see in the darkest places of life.

Your list of desires is probably lasered upon your heart as well. No one scripts your heart's desires; instead, they are imprinted on your heart over time. With the lights on or off you see what you dream and live what you visualize. My physical sight might not be restored this side of eternity unless there is a miracle or major medical breakthrough. Yet, pictures are imprinted in my heart I will never forget.

They help me see when tears of sadness derail my thinking. My heart is full of picture perfect moments and long glances of times past.

Sadly, many only select their failures and losses to imprint on their subconscious. They picture what could have been and look to find some rhyme or reason. They are continually distracted by the past failures that loom in the rear view mirror of their life, instead of focusing their attention through the wide windshield in front of them. Their negative filter of failure, regret, and loss smother the possibilities of this present moment. The result is something more permeating than blindness: a skewed view and a distorted perspective.

Zealous eye specialists were determined to help save the impaired vision of my left eye because it was too late for my right one. To do so would involve an extensive surgery with accompanying risk and uncertainty. Yet the doctors were confident they could delay the inevitable—total blindness. It was one of the hardest decisions of my life. Beyond the risks, I knew I would be totally blind for a season due to bandages and a prolonged time of healing. Manmade blindness was the last thing I wanted. For thirty long days I struggled with disconcerting thoughts, tears, prayers, and counsel before I made my decision. The doctors pressed me to act quickly while there was still time.

While contemplating my options, everything I could see had more value and beauty. With the little eyesight I had left I vividly remember one afternoon observing a peaceful groomed lawn with twenty-eight mighty oak trees nestled on two acres. The flowers were in full bloom, ants were on the move, and the lawn was painted with life in variegated shades of green. Sounds of birds filled a pastel blue sky. I studied the huge trees and the changing color of leaves. Up close the tree bark was incredibly intricate. I laughed as I watched the squirrels run with their cheeks stuffed with acorns as they prepared for the change of seasons. Nature had a new look. Those thirty days of indecision were a gift to my senses as I was surprisingly awakened to the beauty surrounding me.

Suddenly, my peaceful observations were interrupted by a strange sound. I heard an odd thud in the yard. I moved my head toward the direction of the bizarre noise. I called for Tony to come quickly because I wanted to know what just happened. A motionless squirrel lay next to the tree trunk. I thought he must be dead. The twenty-five foot fall looked to be fatal for one apparently blind squirrel, who did not look where he stepped. Then the groggy animal stood slowly and staggered toward the tree. Dazed and weak, the injured squirrel started to climb the tall oak at a reduced pace. Chuckling, Tony told me that the squirrel had evidently lost more than his balance. His bushy tale was missing. Obviously, this little guy had been through a lot already.

Weary of my tormenting indecision I made the call to the hospital and agreed to the vitrectomy eye surgery. My decision was largely based on the counsel of a physician who was a good friend. We would leave early the next morning for Chicago where the surgery would be performed.

I decided to imprint something else in my heart for the uncertain days ahead. I asked my family to come into the makeshift inner sanctum of our cozy family room. Then I directed my children to stand side by side in birth order. Next, I asked my husband to stand at the beginning of the lineup. No one resisted. A solemn stillness blanketed the room as the children stood quietly and watched in wonder. Their ages at the time were 19, 16, 14, 4, and 2.

Staring into my husband's eyes I was profoundly aware of all the challenges we had overcome together on the pathway of our life. I knew our journey was not over, but we both felt anxious. As I held Tony's face in my hands, I saw more than my handsome mate. His gorgeous eyes were crystal blue and framed by soft laugh lines that hinted of good times, which had eased our hardships. His endearing loyalty and faithfulness had never failed me. No man had ever loved a woman like the man whose face I now held. I wondered how I could ever be the wife he needed and deserved.

Drinking in his look of abiding love, the tears rolled off my cheeks. Our determined fight for our miracle family had been costly. Since exchanging our wedding vows our love for life and family had never wavered. I remembered our first Christmas morning as husband and wife when blindness first threatened our future. He had held me tightly as I cried, boldly declaring, "We will not retreat!" Those words were still my compass: My husband was the one to set me on the course I now ran. What an incredible picture of covenant love. His faith and steadfast commitment had never wavered through every hardship and trauma. His enduring love knew no end. My faithful husband still admired me with eyes filled with compassion. I knew I must never lose sight of this portrait of Tony layered in my heart, now crowded with fear and anxiety.

Anna was next. The face of our firstborn was tender and full of innocence. The years had softened the sharp edges of our first memories of brave little Anna, who miraculously lived against all odds. Born with seven complications, transferred from one hospital to another, and the doctor ready to write her death certificate, Anna was a miracle. I remembered the day when every other infant in the neonatal ward had perished and she alone survived. Leaning over her isolette, with tubes in her little body and monitors beeping, I whispered over and over to her, "Choose life, Anna." Her earliest days as a fighter had prepared her to be my right arm. Through her consistent strength and responsible ways she had been the help I needed to raise our family. I could never have mothered her siblings without Anna's priceless assistance and her watchful eye. Gazing into her innocent eyes, Anna looked back at me with eyes of deep love. The hallmarks of her servant leadership and generous heart made her wise beyond her age. Her love for me was fathomless. I wondered if I had ever sufficiently thanked her for all she had done for our family. And now, how much more responsibility would fall on her young shoulders? Knowing Anna's childhood had been cut short due to my infirmity tore this mother's heart in two. I wanted to protect and shield her. My one consolation was my silent hope that all Anna had endured would better equip her for her ultimate assignment in life. Tears clouded both our eyes as I held her sweet face.

Next, I slowly took the face of Lindey, our second daughter, into my hands. Her initial arrival left us all waiting since she was a preemie and had to stay an extra week in the hospital until she was ready to grace her world. Her sweet playful ways and her attempt to say big words at an early age made us laugh, giving us a taste of the entertainment she would bring to our home. Her love for fashion and shoes from a toddler to a teen never changed. Her thoughts were insightful, her life was fun, and everyone was a potential friend. I carefully studied her beautiful face reflecting on her graceful ways. She was trained as a classical ballerina, which allowed her to gracefully float into a room while the rest of us often stumbled into the same place. Lindey's deep blue eyes and dark features only revealed her outward beauty; but it was her winsome walk, humorous wit, and inward beauty, which brought joy to our family. As I looked into her face, I remembered the doctor who bullied me seventeen years earlier to choose between Lindey's unborn life and my eyesight. She was not merely our treasure, but a gift to the world. Looking deep into her soul through her eyes I imprinted her smile of beauty in the chambers of my heart.

Of all the births, Holly's was the easiest. I vividly remember the nurse's placement of her at the window of the nursery with her beautiful thick dark hair and a bow on her head. She was our miracle gift two weeks before Christmas on her grandmother's 50th birthday. Now she stood patiently waiting for me to hold her face as I worked down the line. Her strong features hinted of her determined ways and leadership potential. The two of us had often clashed into each other's stubbornness because we were cut of the same cloth. Yet now, her beauty and sweet countenance rested peacefully in my hands. We mirrored each other. Holly's smile could melt the hardest heart, and when she sang, her astonishing voice could raise the roof. She had the potential to follow in my footsteps as a recording artist and traveling vocalist. My kindred and beloved daughter watched me with tears. I hoped she could learn life's lessons in a kinder, gentler way than I had. Her face seemed surprisingly vulnerable in my hands, as I soaked in her expression, while more tears rolled down my face. It was unmistakable: she was a next generation leader. That I could see clearly. Her bright future helped diminish the shadows I faced.

I paused before moving down the line looking back to the original family. That's how I referred to the first three daughters, as our next two children were a special golden bonus package after a nine year intermission. Borrowing an idea from the twenty-third Psalm, I often called our two little ones Goodness and Mercy, because I knew they would follow us all the days of our lives. They had experienced a different childhood and mother than the first three children. Most likely they were convinced they had many mothers. Their older sisters hovered over them and attended to all their needs. Consequently, Lydia and Connor were inseparable. I failed to hold back the tears when I saw my two little ones standing erect, waiting their turn. Leaning over them, I took a deep breath and tried to imagine what these two small children would look like as young adults.

I remembered the surprise of Lydia Ellison's arrival and how it gave our home ecstatic joy. Each of us eagerly waited our turn to hold our treasured Lady Lydia. Now she was soon to be five years old and already displayed uncommon leadership. She gladly took charge over her brother relishing her self-appointed older sister role. In fact, once she saved her brother's life by successfully fishing him out of the swimming pool before an adult could get there. Already, she walked with an authoritative step. No one doubted her command of life. I often said over her, "Lydia, you will rock nations one day." Regardless of that prophecy her little eyes and smile before me now reminded me she was a mere child. Of all our children Lydia was the only baby I was allowed to hold after childbirth. She snuggled to me as I sang over her, "You are my sunshine, my only sunshine." I now strained to imagine her as a grown woman with her captivating smile and her prankster ways. Undoubtedly, her strength would be needed in the future with a mommy who was less than all she should need. Tears streamed down my face as I held hers. I lingered longingly, not wanting to miss the years ahead. Lydia was oblivious to any obstacles that threatened our future together. My "abnormal" was her normal, and she saw no obstacle in her way. I wanted the same.

And then, there was Connor. We had been thrilled at the gift of a son after four lovely daughters. We called him Connor Boy or Connor Man from the beginning. I remembered well the non-stop laughter my husband and I shared in the doctor's waiting room after the sonogram convincingly announced that we were about to have a boy. Though accused by his sisters that I loved him more, the truth is that sons are indeed different than daughters. Connor was two years old and adorable. He was the small version of his daddy with similar expressions and mannerisms. He loved to cuddle and always gave big hugs. My heart could barely stand to think of not seeing his face clearly. Even then it was hazy. I held my son's face tightly thanking God for my last gift. As I looked deep into his eyes I pictured how he would carry on our family's name. I tried to imagine him as a husband and daddy one day. His frame and coordination suggested a future in sports. "Ball" had been Connor's first spoken word. I wondered now how many of his baseball and soccer games I would actually see. I stroked his little face with longings too deep to express. Connor started to wiggle away, unaware of the gravity of the moment. He just knew he was secure, because we all were together. He was clueless I could not see.

I looked back with a concentrated attempt to burn into my memory what our children looked like in the event I never saw them again.

When I left for Chicago early the following morning my heart was full. I was grateful for the vivid mental images of those I loved, because my eyes would remain patched for an extended period of time after the surgery. That first major surgery lasted nearly five hours. Then, two more intricate surgeries were performed on my eyes in the following year.

One year passed before I returned to the surgeon's office. The surgeon quietly looked over my records and thoroughly examined my eyes. Then he sat silently for several moments before turning to face us. As he tenderly touched my shoulder, with a tone of sorrow in his voice, he said, "Gail. I'm sorry. There is no hope."

Tears gushed down my cheeks as I proclaimed, "I leave this office in hope. No man can take your hope." My worst fear had been realized. It now seemed that I had lived the past year in vain. Had I merely been a medical guinea pig on which some aggressive surgeons had tested their latest theories? Even though my eyesight was still broken, the imprints of my children in my heart still reflected brilliant color and enduring hope.

Most live life based only on what they see with their eyes. The dreams they carry in their heart are frequently blurred by difficult challenges. Maintaining a clear vision is the key to overcoming obstacles in your life. I am not in denial, but I am certainly not stuck in my dark crisis and dimming light. I choose to see beyond my visual acuity and position myself for great days ahead.

Have you considered taking the faces of your own children in your hands and imprint those lives deep in your heart? What will you see when you study that priceless face? If you could see into their future, what words of encouragement could best prepare them for it? Then, with those faces imprinted in your heart, perhaps some of your own struggles and shortcomings will be easier to cast off. Remember that your life is also imprinted on the heart of the next generation. Your children and grandchildren are looking for authentic lives to emulate, and they long for a heritage to embrace.

Discover lasting motivation by imprinting those closest to you on your mind and heart. Make an imprint now. You're not stuck—you've been positioned.

YIELD

When my husband and I were first married we lived in a small community in the Midwest. We purchased a home outside a city of 100,000 people in a nearby town that was surrounded by farmland. Our first daughter was born the previous summer, and we were eager to conquer the world. Our small backyard bumped up to a larger piece of property connected to a field. Our dear neighbors, Max and Lois, lived there. They were like parents to us, and they frequently brought us big hugs, fresh produce, and helpful tips for rural living.

One day Max came over with a most unexpected offer. He wanted to "loan" us a portion of his land that would extend our backyard. Max then offered to plow the land so we could have a garden of our own. We were excited because we were living in Illinois where the rich topsoil is known as black gold. Fertile fields surrounded us, and now we were going to get a piece of the action.

Max plowed a generous plot, forty feet by eighty feet. As he tilled the soil he suggested we go to town and pick out the seeds we wanted to plant. Tony and I were excited about the potential of living off the land. We dreamed of growing our own produce and laying up canned goods for the winter months to come.

Our small town of 1,400 people had a small business district, including a hardware store that carried a variety of seeds. Tony and I selected packets of seeds we loved, like tomatoes, sweet corn, broccoli, carrots, and more. My husband loves radishes. We bought those as well. I found some pretty packages of plants I had never heard of, but loved the pictures, so I grabbed some. We added other vegetables that would make a garden full, including cucumbers and zucchini. The joy and excitement of planting our seed blinded us to what came next.

We maximized the few hours we had before dusk and began to plant our seeds. My husband stretched a string across the width of the garden to make sure the rows were straight. We evenly spaced our planted seeds so our garden looked aesthetically pleasing. It gave plenty of room for plant growth. The potential was obvious, but unbeknownst to us, our newly planted garden was about to teach us some powerful life lessons.

The challenge of any garden is waiting for seeds to grow. Every day we would look out our kitchen window wondering how our garden fared. In a few short weeks there was evidence of growth. The rainfall that season was more than adequate; every variety of vegetable grew faster than we expected.

Gardening 101 quickly taught us there is more to a harvest than just planting seeds. Everything green in a garden is not necessarily edible. It was my first introduction to weeds. I never considered there would be competition for the soil's nutrients. These intruders caused us to make another purchase—a hoe. Soon we felt like we were slaves to what we had planted. Every night we tended the garden with endless hoeing and weed pulling.

We didn't just plant one tomato plant; we planted dozens. In fact, we had four different varieties of tomatoes, and each plant had to be supported with stakes and wire. If one cucumber mound seemed sufficient, then we thought two would be even better. Sweet corn is a must during the summer, but we had not thought about how many corn seeds would be enough for one small family and a few friends. We both loved green beans, so we wanted to make sure we would have enough left over to can. In our zeal we planted twelve forty-foot rows of green beans—480 feet of beans. When I tell this story to live audiences, a collective gasp nearly takes the air out of the room. If you have any gardening experience, you know the green beans alone were excessive, even ridiculous.

Some evenings I would catch a glimpse of our neighbors smiling at us and waving. I thought they were just friendly, until I noticed several other neighbors were watching, smiling, and waving. I'm sure we provided great entertainment in the neighborhood that summer, two city kids who did not have a clue what they were doing with a fertile garden plot. Little did we know the harvest was about to overtake our entire summer.

Lettuce was our first big crop, but I had no clue what to do with it. It seemed odd to go to the grocery store to buy vegetables to put in our lettuce salad while we waited on everything else to finish growing. But we did. Then, seemingly overnight, our garden erupted. The work was endless. Was this, we wondered, what was called a bumper crop?

The zucchini and cucumber mounds alone had outlandish yields. We ate what we could and gave away plenty to our family and friends. I made zucchini bread, which was costly after you figure in the sugar, oil, flour and eggs. Zucchini loaves were all over the counters, and the kitchen was constantly hot because of using our oven all day long. It seemed treasonous when I suggested to my husband we eat out, but we needed a break.

We looked forward to our next selection for our salad bar. Soon, the corn was ripe for picking. Our suntans were golden while we shucked four forty-foot rows of corn in the scorching sun. After supplying the neighborhood with ears of corn and enjoying fresh corn for every meal, we knew we had to do something fast.

My Granny sent us a gift to celebrate our harvest. Looking back she was probably laughing too, but on the phone she encouraged us to keep up the good work. Her gift was a pressure cooker. We put it into immediate use.

Freezer bags and a vacuum sealer were purchased next. The kitchen was a mess with sticky timers, billows of steam, blanching paraphernalia, and our assembly line of two packaging the super sweet corn. It tasted like candy. Our next challenge was where to put it all. When you are young and naive you discover Sears will sell you anything on credit, so we bought a freezer. It filled immediately with bags of corn and loaves of zucchini bread.

The next expense was canning jars—several cases in all, with rings and lids, too.

Tomatoes are my absolute favorite. I never realized how many different varieties there were, not to mention all their different colors. We ate tomatoes till the canker sores developed. Again we offered food to the neighborhood and still had plenty to can. Tomato juice and salsa were our favorite. The catsup was runny but could be used in some recipe, I was sure.

Our idea of living off the land was met with new unexpected expenses. If it wasn't the oven adding heat to the kitchen, it was the pressure cooker going non-stop. Different recipes screamed for fresh vegetables of some kind. Broccoli casseroles; corn casseroles; fried tomatoes; mashed, baked and twice baked potatoes were just a sampling of our summer cuisine. But each new cooking venture required expensive ingredients to enhance them, and the costs were mounting.

We became obsessed with reading garden recipe books by Betty Crocker and Good Housekeeping magazines while we waited for the water to boil and the pressure cooker to whistle. Clearly, we were in over our heads. We marveled how simple and routine our grandmothers had made gardening look.

One night I served garden fresh broccoli to my husband. It is his favorite vegetable. But no one had warned me to soak the broccoli in salt water before cooking it. I didn't know that little green worms might otherwise be part of the recipe. During dinner I felt proud of our accomplishments and boasted that everything on the table was from our garden. Then my husband innocently inquired, "What are these little green things on my plate?" I didn't have the heart to ask if he ate them for extra protein.

Neighbors continued to watch while we tackled our robust field of green beans. Night after night we placed mounting piles of freshly picked green beans on our patio deck and spent our evenings snapping them. I sent Tony back to the hardware store for several more cases of canning jars.

The first green bean harvest resulted in our canning two hundred quarts of green beans. The second picking was just as plentiful and we gave it away to people we didn't even know. By the third picking I didn't even care and told Tony, "Let it all rot on the vine!" I was done. Our kitchen counters were filled with quart jars of green beans until my husband built a pantry next to our new freezer. We drew from that supply over the next five years.

If that summer wasn't embarrassing enough, I am even more embarrassed to say that we have never gardened since. However, we have never stopped sowing seeds.

Beyond the joy of planting seeds, whether in a field or into another's life, the question remains, "Have you considered what you will reap?" Whether you impact a nation, a generation, or a neighborhood, you must remember that there is a yield to your life's efforts.

I retold that story of our first and only garden at a board meeting of business leaders who were carefully considering a building program. The layout of their current campus was comfortable and manageable. However, if they were to efficiently meet the needs of growing clientele, they would need to expand. Figuratively speaking, they would have to buy some freezer space and build a pantry, if they were to adequately contain all the projected growth. They were wisely considering the cost of that growth to better develop a contingency plan.

Dormant seeds sitting in a package placed safely in a cabinet will never produce anything. I once had a package of Texas bluebonnet seeds. I loved the picture on the outside of the package. However, the picture only hints of their potential. Intentionally planting and nurturing my seed is the mandate for a bountiful harvest. So it is with our own lives. We know our lives have great potential and that our dreams are honorable. But, it will take intentional effort to see our dreams become reality.

Nothing is more beautiful in the springtime landscape of Texas than the bluebonnets growing wildly alongside the highways. The phenomenon of cars pulled alongside the roadways is part of the culture when these beauties make their annual appearance. The number of photographs taken of families and children during this season is as profuse as the flowers themselves. The bluebonnet has been the Texas state flower since 1901. They naturally proliferated throughout much of the state. It is said that bluebonnets and other Texas wild flowers made an impact on young Lady Bird Johnson. She grew up to become the first lady of the White House when her husband, Lyndon Baines Johnson, was the 36th President of the United States. Lady Bird's love of beautiful landscapes and environments led to the first major legislative campaign ever launched by a first lady. The Highway Beautification Act of 1965 is also referred to as Lady Bird's Bill. Since that time long ago the amount of seedlings and flowers that have been intentionally planted has expanded our nation's natural beauty beyond imagination.

Lady Bird Johnson was born Claudia Alta Taylor. The nickname "Lady Bird stuck after a nurse called her that as a baby. It wasn't long after marrying LBJ and joining the political scene that Lady Bird displayed her obvious talent as an entrepreneur. Her enterprising endeavors were incredibly successful because she made intelligent investments. She turned her own modest inheritance into a successful congressional campaign for her husband. Later, she bought a radio station and a television station. Those investments eventually turned the Johnsons into millionaires.

Seeds face natural challenges to their destiny. Sometimes the environment is too hot, too cold, too dry, or too wet. They have a constant need for the right quantity of water, nutrients, and light. Sometimes, this balance is not well maintained by nature. But in most cases, plants find a way to produce nonetheless. Those who tend the seeds and the resulting plants always maintain an expectation of growth. A bountiful harvest is the anticipated end. And, as a result, others always benefit from the yield.

You may think it impossible to grow anything in your life right now. It's not true. You may think you are stuck in a hostile environment where your personal growth and development are hindered, but don't overlook a simple fact. Your very life is a seed, and in spite of unpredictable conditions, you can flourish. Others will benefit.

I recall a picture I once saw of a mountainside with jagged rock edges. Amazingly, a tree grew in the crack in the side of the mountain where there was hardly any soil, let alone fertile topsoil. Still, there were enough essential elements hidden in that barren place in which a random seed took root. The determined seedling grew in the midst of adverse conditions to the wonderment of all who encountered it. As it grew in stature the emerging tree provided a landing place for birds and shade for reptiles that lived in the crevasses of the rocks. Truly that tenacious tree looked out of place, but it is a picture of a seed's natural quest to grow even in unfavorable environments.

The early childhood story of my friend, James Robison, reminds me of that resilient mountainside tree. His beginning was anything but ideal. His mother was a practical nurse who served as a caregiver in the homes of elderly patients. At the age of forty, her client's alcoholic son raped her. This was how James was conceived. She sought an abortion, but her doctor said no. Unable to juggle caring for her newborn and maintaining her livelihood, she put an ad in the Houston paper looking for a Christian couple to provide a stable home for her newborn son. James ended up in the home of a local pastor.

When James was five his mother took him back into her humble home, but their lives were far from comfortable. Absolute poverty is how James described it. They had a rough life. When James was around fourteen, his alcoholic father came back in their home and nearly killed his mother. In self-defense James almost killed him. The father was arrested and taken away. James eventually expressed his gratefulness that he had not killed the man. He soon returned to the home of the pastor where he later met his wife, Betty.

James and Betty married in 1963 and by 1980 had three children, a television outreach, and influence in social, religious, and political spheres. James has spoken to more than twenty million people in several hundred citywide evangelistic outreaches. Currently, he leads an organization that reaches fifty nations on six continents. Throughout Africa they help feed 400,000 children weekly in crisis areas and assist with school feeding programs to encourage school attendance and education. According to reports from the field they have helped save the lives of millions of starving children. Fruit and vegetable farms and food processing plants are also part of the scope. Medical clinics and orphanages round out a variety of ways they reach into the lives of many. They have also drilled more than 4,000 fresh water wells in forty nations. James is a significant friend to those in desperate situations.

The yield of his mother's courageous decision is the vast harvest that continues to impact the entire world. The sterling character developed within James in the hard places of his early life continues to pave the way for others to get a foothold on life today. His voice of hope gives comfort in the scorching heat of life's most impossible situations.

Prepare for the yield of your life. Conditions will rarely be perfect, but persevere. You will be amazed how your dreams can grow to fruition from seeds planted in obscure places and even under undesirable circumstances. The faltering dreams of others will be nourished by your determination to break through the rocky limitations of your circumstances.

Keep sowing your seeds. Keep cultivating your garden to weed out unwanted seeds of doubt. You just might be on the cusp of a bumper crop. Work to implant your life in the rich soil of visionary wisdom, uncompromising character, and true inspiration. There's a life to live and a harvest to enjoy. The fruit of your labor will enrich many. You're not stuck—you've been positioned.

DO IT

knew that my parents would love Zig Ziglar and his dear wife, Jean, from the moment I first had the pleasure of meeting them. In short order the two couples became close friends and both were active members of the same church in Dallas. On Sunday afternoons, I often found them sharing lunch and loads of laughter with many other friends from their large Sunday school class.

One particular Sunday I had just returned to Dallas after speaking at a convention in the area. I had the idea that I could catch my parents during the lunch hour to check on them and give a short recap of my recent engagement. They have always been my biggest cheerleaders and are eager to hear my reports. Imagine my delight to find them seated with my next-favorite pair of cheerleading champions, the Ziglars.

Room was made for me to join them at their table, already filled with eight couples. I sat across from Zig, who, like a Poppa, leaned in and listened attentively. I quickly rattled off the highlights of my most recent speaking engagements in my typical animated style. When I finished Zig surprised me when he said, "Gail, you inspire me."

In awe, I gazed into the face of my dear friend who had so faithfully cheered me on to new heights. His was the voice that motivated the corporate world and beyond. My heart overflowed with gratitude to think that Zig Ziglar took such a personal interest in my life's journey. In that pivotal moment time seemed to stand still. What a paradox, when I also had a keen sense that years were passing swiftly.

The faces of those nearest me faded away as I focused on my role model across the table. I drank in the precious moment and yet wondered how many times I would be given such an opportunity. I moved the place setting in front of me off to the side and slid my arm slowly across the table toward my dear friend. Unaware that Zig had his eye on me he did the same. Our hands met and clasped in the middle of the table. I said, "Mr. Ziglar, I want to take a word of encouragement to my generation like you did to yours."

Zig reminded me again that when you have a word of encouragement you always have something to give. This landmark never left me from the first time I heard him say those words years previously. That admonition has become the theme of my lifestyle. He went on to speak into my life. I took each word to heart. Then he said emphatically, "Do it."

I made one more request of my legendary friend. "Would you pray over me?"

Zig did not hesitate. We released our grasp. The moment was over. A monumental life exchange had taken place. Only then did I become aware that we had witnesses who had silently observed the interchange with great interest.

A gentleman seated to my left asked, "What just happened?" Another man who sat catty-cornered from me was profoundly impacted. He leaned in and asked, "What did we just witness?" Surprised that our moment seemed significant to anyone else, I suddenly realized I had just been given permission to soar.

To this very day, *"Do it!"* still resounds in my soul. I was commissioned to influence my own generation with motivation, encouragement, and inspiration. Best of all, I was given permission to live my dream. I recount this story to make a point: It really doesn't matter if I become as famous as Zig Ziglar or even get close to becoming the kind of motivational icon to *my* generation that Zig was to his. One thing alone matters: Do it!

My message to you now is one and the same: *Do it!*

Live your dream. Expand your vision. Loose yourself from the constraints of your comfort zone. Soar to greater heights. Explore new horizons. Implement real change. Yes you can. You're not stuck. *Do it!*

Refuse to be your own worst enemy. Stop underestimating the power of your life and its influence. Give yourself permission to impact your world and make a difference. The voice of "can't" must go. Just get up and *do it!*

I remember once when Windsor Hope, our infant grand-daughter, was staying with us. Her heart's desire was mobility and her new focus was learning to crawl. We delighted in giving her our applause each time she inched and plodded across the floor. With a single-minded focus Windsor would crawl as far as her little arms and legs would support her before dropping and rolling to her desired location. It was just the beginning of her newfound talents. Life is changing rapidly for little Windsor. And, it will change for her entire family as well, as she continues her quest to reach beyond her limits to move ever faster and more efficiently to her targeted desti-nation. Each plateau will present her with other challenges, and each small victory will bring her newfound joy. Meanwhile, her success is assured, because she is surrounded by so many who are committed to her growth and development.

You need a similar support system. If your friends aren't capable or willing to provide the support you need, then get new friends. Do not be held back by visionless people who might feel uncomfortable with your new success. Diligently search for resources to encourage your growth and stretch your capabilities. Devour books, attend seminars, and enlist coaches who share your vision.

Be warned: this lifestyle is addictive.

I am reminded of a story of a treasure given to someone who buried it for fear it might be lost. What he feared most happened the moment the first shovel of dirt covered the treasure. With the treasure safely buried, it offered neither hope nor promise to change his life or the lives of those in his sphere of influence. Others, with a treasure of the same value, invested it and it multiplied.

Similarly, the treasure of *your* life is not to be stuck underground beneath the dirt of fear. It must be invested. Admittedly, investments have risks, but without the risk the potential is untapped. No goals are accomplished by stagnant living. No battles are won by unimplemented strategies. No returns are earned on investments never made. I'm talking about more than a catchy motto or clever marketing campaign to increase your client base. I'm talking about a mindset that will bring about a lifestyle change and lasting results. The moment you fully comprehend that you are strategically positioned, and *not* stuck, you will live life totally different.

No longer wait for the best to come to you, but tap your own capacities and potential and bring your best to your world. Your view will suddenly broaden with limitless possibilities as you learn to treat each new day as a gift. Each assignment is an addition to your resume; each failure is a place from which to launch a new strategy; and each delay contains within it another opportunity to reflect, as you wait in hope. More is set in motion by the *attitude* you embrace than you realize.

Ultimately, your belief system will determine your course and what resources are placed at your disposal. If you only believe in yourself and your own ability you will eventually experience your own limitations. But in contrast, if you believe in a team effort your sphere of influence will expand in ways you could not accomplish by yourself. Add prayer to the equation and new dimensions can develop beyond your imagination as His strategies and wisdom are welcomed into the process.

You have this time in history. Embrace the challenges. Shrug off the setbacks. Give yourself to the day at hand. You can—you must—do it!

Go ahead and live. Hold nothing back.

You're not stuck—you've been positioned.

Attributions

CHAPTER 1 - POSITIONED
Page 4 Elie Wiesel, *Open Heart*
http://www.biography.com/people/elie-wiesel-9530714

CHAPTER 3 - 50 YARD LINE
Page 10   Michael Jordan
http://www.biography.com/people/michael-jordan-9358066

Page 10 Lucille Ball
http://www.biography.com/people/lucille-ball-9196958

Page 10 Harrison Ford
http://www.biography.com/people/harrison-ford-9298701

Page 10 Denzel Washington
http://www.biography.com/people/denzel-washington-9524687

Page 11 Steve Jobs
http://allaboutstevejobs.com/bio/shortbio.php

Page 11 Henry Ford
http://www.planetmotivation.com/never-quit.html

Page 11 Colonel Sanders
http://franchises.about.com/od/mostpopularfranchises/a/colonel-sanders.htm

Page 11 2014 World Cup
http://www.cbsnews.com/news/world-cup-2014-germany-vs-argentina-final/

Page 12 Kurt Warner
http://www.biography.com/people/kurt-warner-519490#switching-teams

CHAPTER 4 – HOPE
Page 18 Bob Hope
http://www.biography.com/people/bob-hope-9343481#king-of-media

Page 18 John Steinbeck, *Once There Was a War*
http://www.americainwwii.com/articles/bob-hope-and-the-road-to-gi-joe/

CHAPTER 5 – FOG
Page 24 George Prince Ferry
http://www.nola.com/175years/index.ssf/2011/12/1976_dozens_were_killed_in_fer.html

Page 26 John F. Kennedy, Jr.
http://www.jfklibrary.org/JFK/JFK-in-History/November-22-1963-Death-of-the-President.aspx
http://www.history.com/this-day-in-history/jfk-jr-killed-in-plane-crash

CHAPTER 6- GRATEFUL

Page 31 Dennis Prager, *Happiness is a Serious Problem*
http://Dennisprager.com

Page 37 Megan Moyers McMillan, MD. Used by permission.

CHAPTER 9- BEYOND

Page 57   William Ligon, as told to the author. Used by permission.

Page 60   Farris Wilks, as told to the author. Used by permission.

Page 60   David Sposato, as told to the author. Used by permission.

CHAPTER 10 - CHOICES

Page 63 Prime Minister Golda Meir
http://www.britannica.com/biography/Golda-Meir

Page 64   Rosa Parks
http://www.americaslibrary.gov/jb/modern/jb_modern_parks_1.html

Page 67 John Wilson, as told to the author. Used by permission.

Page 70 Bob McEwen, as told to the author. Used by permission.

CHAPTER 11 – STALL

Page 76 Chuck Yeager
http://www.wired.com/2009/10/1014yeager-breaks-mach-1/

Page 76   Edgar Albert Guest
Somebody Said it Couldn't be Done

CHAPTER 12 – MOVIE

Page 83 Nic Vujicic
http://www.lifewithoutlimbs.org

CHAPTER 14- RELEVANT

Page 93 Hurricane Mitch
http://www.history.com/topics/hurricane-mitch

Page 97 *The Guardian - Bible Became Most Popular Book in Norway* 2011
http://www.theguardian.com/books/2012/jan/03/bible-2011-bestseller-norway

ATTRIBUTIONS

Page 97 David Barton, *Wallbuilders,* Aledo, Texas

Page 98 Ben Carson, MD

CHAPTER 15 – WELLS

Page 101 Booker T. Washington
http://americanradioworks.publicradio.org/features/sayitplain/btwashington.html

Page 104 John Quincy Adams
http://dutyisours.com/duty.htm

Page 104 Proverbs 14:33, Genesis26:13

Page 106 Norman Williams
http://www.secrettenerife.co.uk/2004/03/on-this-day-1977-runway-collision.shtml

CHAPTER 17- ROOF

Page 119 Allison Levine
http://www.markets.businessclubsamerica.com/alison-levine-s-150.html

CHAPTER 19- FLIGHT

Page 133 Jeanette Graves and Ken Graves, as told to the author. Used by permission.

CHAPTER 20- DELAY

Page 137 Joseph Bell and Gene Weingarten
http://www.joshuabell.com/news/pulitzer-prize-winning-washington-post-feature

Page 140 Mike Huckabee
From *Hope to Higher Ground*

Page 142 Scott Turner, as told to the author. Used by permission

Page 143 Santina Stearns, as told to the author. Used by permission

Page 143 Peter Schreiber, *In My Seat; A Pilots Story* from Sept. 10th -11th

Page 144 September 11, 2001
http://www.britannica.com/event/September-11-attacks

Page 146 Big Thompson Canyon, Colorado
https://www.coloradoinfo.com/estespark/bigthompsoncanyon

CHAPTER 23- MIDNIGHT

Page 161 Times Square Ball
http://www.timessquarenyc.org/events/new-years-eve/about-the-new-years-eve-ball/history-of-the-new-years-eve-ball/index.aspx#.VX8bt1wbBsM

Page 164 Psalm 30:5
Weeping may last for the night, but joy comes in the morning.

Page 167 Star Spangled Banner
http://www.history.com/this-day-in-history/key-pens-star-spangled-banner

CHAPTER 24- CRUCIBLE

Page 169 Leslie and Bob Brewer, as told to the author. Used by permission

Page 170 Kami and Clint Collins, as told to the author, Used by permission

Page 171 Chicago Fire
http://www.history.com/topics/great-chicago-fire

Page 172 Eagle Bronze, Inc. as told to the author, Used by permission

CHAPTER 25- PUZZLED

Page 179 Laura and Joshua Huene, *String of Pearls*
http://stringofpearlsonline.org

Page 181 Rebekah Mitchell, *Mommies Enduring Neonatal Death*
http://www.mend.org/support/

Page 181 Tracey Terasas, *Remembering Wyatt Dale Water Safety Awareness*
http://rememberingwyattdale.org

Page 181 Jay Dan Gumm, Forgiven Felons
http://forgivenfelons.org

Page 182 Dave Roever, Operation Warrior RECONnect
http://roeverfoundation.org/project.php?id=12

Page 182 Joni Eareckson Tada, Joni and Friends Inc.
http://www.joniandfriends.org

CHAPTER 27- YIELD

Page 198 Lady Bird Johnson
http://www.lbjlibrary.org/lyndon-baines-johnson/lady-bird-johnson

Page 199 James Robison
http://lifetoday.org/about-life/james-and-betty-robison/

Gail McWILLIAMS

Gail McWilliams is a seasoned speaker, author, and national radio host who engages her audiences with challenge, humor and life-changing inspiration. Her courageous and gripping story of gradually losing her eyesight while having her children is the backdrop to her life-message of vision that sees no limits. Gail says, "In my darkest hour vision was birthed, and when you have vision you can see in the darkest places of life." She is humorous, challenging, and unforgettable. Gail exudes hope, vision, and the ability to see beyond any obstacle. Her inspiration and motivation help people take steps toward their personal dreams and toward a high sense of purpose.

BOOK GAIL TODAY
FOR YOUR NEXT EVENT!

888.270.0182
info@GailMcWilliams.com

www.GailMcWilliams.com